99

HOBSON'S -CHOICE-

Recollections of a North Country Engineman

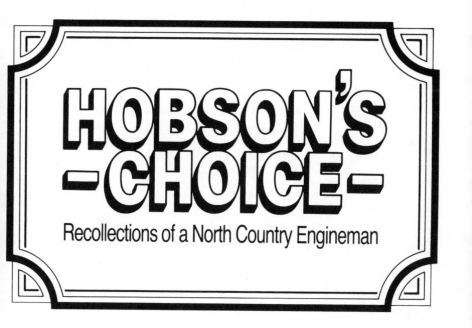

HOBSON'S -CHOICE-

Recollections of a North Country Engineman

DENNIS HOBSON

Oxford Publishing Co.

ISBN 0-86093-370-9

Typesetting by:
Aquarius Typesetting Services, New Milton, Hants.
Colin Powell Typesetting & Design, Bournemouth, Dorset.

Printed in Great Britain by:
Biddles Ltd., Guildford and Kings Lynn.

Published by
Oxford Publishing Co.
Link House
West Street
POOLE, Dorset

British Library Cataloguing in Publication Data
Hobson's Choice: recollections of a North Country
engineman. — (Reminiscences)
1. British Rail. London Midland Region
2. Railroads — England, Northern
I. Title II. Series
625.2′61′0924   HE3019.N6/

Acknowledgements

I would like to thank my wife and son who have given me their support in this project, Vivienne Hopkinson for typing my manuscript and the gentlemen who have kindly supplied me with photographic material.
Specific thanks to Rex Kennedy, Editor, and Noel Bell, Publisher, who have always been at hand to advise me.

Contents

ILLUSTRATIONS

Between pages 32 and 33

ILLUSTRATIONS

Between pages 64 and 65

Preface

This is the author's account of his service on the railways in the days of steam. It consists of a number of random recollections and anecdotes, spanning almost twenty years, from when he was taken on by the LMS Railway in 1939, until he left the London Midland Region of British Railways.

He describes in detail many aspects of life on the railways, and the various jobs he did, starting with cleaning the engines and finishing as a passed fireman (acting driver). He describes trips he made, dramas, amusing incidents and some of the tragedies.

Introduction

I have been asked by my family to write my story of life on the railways in the days of steam. They seem to enjoy my reminiscences about that wonderful experience. Believe me, it was an experience, and I feel privileged to have spent a major part of my working life on steam locomotives.

I left the railway company after almost twenty years of service because of constant talk about the closure of Hasland motive power depot. There were to be economic cuts which would inevitably mean that signal boxes, sidings, stations and even locomotive depots would have to go. The old steam shed was already showing signs of neglect, and the whole roof structure had to be removed as it was in danger of falling in. This may have been brought about by subsidence from the local collieries; Grassmoor, Bonds Main, Williamthorpe and Holmewood pits were not so far away.

I sometimes feel that I should have been more adventurous and 'moved on' to another depot. At that time one could have selected some really secure depots. If one of these places advertised for footplate staff, the applicant with the longer period of service would get the position. Should no outsiders apply, the senior man for promotion at that depot would step up. My wife and I had long talks about our future and the possibility of moving home, but we finally decided to stay put and I gave in my notice and secured a job at a local steelworks.

The sad position was that when a man left the railways he lost all his seniority. It was just impossible under those circumstances to go back and try to start at the bottom again. The foreman's last words were 'don't leave now, you are at the top of the tree and have done all the hard work'. But I did leave, and all that is left are memories. I am nearing retirement age now, so bear with me and I will recount how it all began, and forgive me if I don't remember all the correct details.

Chapter One

CLEANING AND A START ON FIRING

I left school at 14 years of age, in 1935. Like a lot of other schoolboys I had a strong desire to get a job on the railways and wrote several times asking 'please, have you any vacancies?'

The thirties were hard years and jobs were few and far between. Imagine my surprise and excitement when, in early 1939, I was asked to go the Hasland motive power depot for an interview. This was like the answer to a prayer; in fact I had given up hope of ever being considered.

Duly arriving for the appointment, I seemed to fit all requirements, was a decent 5ft. 8½ in. tall, but I would have to undergo an eyesight test. This was to be at the local headquarters at Derby. The Company asked for five new entrants for Hasland on that day, and as it turned out I was the second oldest applicant. This meant that if I did get the job my age would make me the second senior of the five new employees. So much depended on having perfect eye-sight, and I must admit that we were all rather scared of failing the test.

On arrival at Derby, we were, in turn, asked to sit in a corridor and were tested for both ordinary and colour vision. In the colours there were green, red, white and yellow, and these were flashed in all sorts of different sequences, the light sometimes becoming smaller in size. We were told afterwards that each colour could be shaded several times, and I would imagine the various sizes of the coloured light were simulated to viewing signals at different distances. We were also shown the Japanese colour vision test book. This was invented by a professor named Ishiara. The book contained several pages of coloured dots. A person with normal colour vision would see a number interposed in the dots; a colour blind person would see a different number or perhaps no number at all. The examiner could, by this method, pick out a colour blind person. The *Ishiara* was certainly a cleverly-constructed book. With great relief and joy we were all told that we had passed the tests and were required to report for duty on the following Monday morning.

However, before continuing with the story, I would like to tell a joke about the eyesight test.

It appears that the doctor-in-charge of eyesight testing had run out of time. He peeped into the waiting-room and noticed a solitary little figure waiting for his test. The doctor was in a hurry to get home as he had an important appointment. Calling the young man into his office he said, 'if you can read the bottom line on that chart on the wall with one eye I will pass you'. The bright young lad had stared hard and long. 'I have got it doctor', he exclaimed

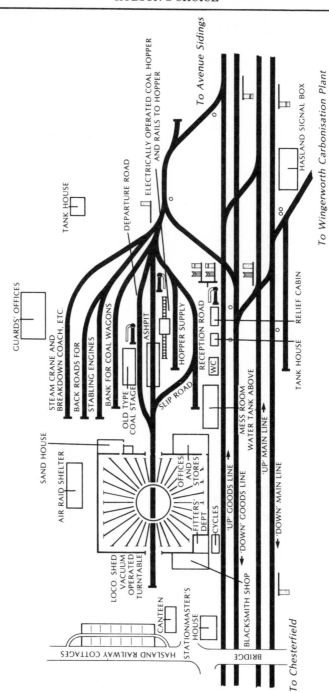

A plan of Hasland motive power depot in the early days.

cheerfully. 'Bembrose and Sons, Printers, Derby'. Oh dear, what powers of observation!

It is sad to say, but out of the five of us who started that day in 1939, there are only two of us left to tell the tale.

Our first job at Hasland involved engine cleaning, which meant getting buckets full of paraffin and some rags. After scraping away the dirt and old grease, we washed the components down with the paraffin and then polished off with the dry rags.

Because it was a dirty job cleaning the motions, etc. inside the framing, we would take turns in our duties. If we were cleaning the outside one day we would swap over the next day with our mates, who were cleaning the inside. We learned to take pride in our engine cleaning and it was said that, when we had finished, the foreman would follow us round with his white handkerchief. If he dirtied it, we would have to start all over again. Our boss was very keen, but not as keen as that, I can assure you.

Other than cleaning engines, of course, there were many other important jobs to do, like helping to empty the ash pits or fill the coal tubs for the engine tenders. All this was good training in the art of using a shovel. We also helped the steam raisers. Most of these 'old codgers' could make a 'dead engine' alive and into a powerful monster in no time at all. These chaps often asked us to do the hard bit; they would show us how to replace or renew damaged firebars, then instruct us how to line the firebox area with coal. It was necessary to completely cover all the firebars with a good layer of coal, then, with a long fire-cleaning type of shovel, gently place several lighted fire lighters all round the firebox. Sometimes, if it was available, we would take shovelfuls of fire from other engines standing nearby, or fetch a barrow load of fire from the sand house fire. This would all help to ignite the coal more quickly. The steam raiser would then put the steam jet handle to the fully open position. After that, all one could do was wait until the fire really took hold. The damper under the engine would be partly open so as to allow air under the fire, with the firebox doors firmly closed. Eventually, smoke would start to roll off the top of the engine chimney and drift out from any gaps around the fire hole doors, often filling the engine cab. It would be foolish at that stage to open the doors, or one would run the risk of being choked with smoke and fumes. After a while, the coal would all be alight and burning merrily. Gradually, the water in the boiler would boil and start to produce steam. As the steam rose in temperature, the jet, which had previously been fully opened, would start to operate. A jet of steam would emerge from the chimney via the blower pipe ring, and the smoke drifting around in the smokebox would be induced to go up the engine chimney in a straight column, and be drawn to the outside of the shed roof by the enormous ventilators. Then the steam raiser could safely open the fire hole doors, check around, and make sure that everything was to his satisfaction. With a steady 60 or 70 pounds of steam pressure on the steam gauge, and plenty of water in the boiler, the damper would be firmly closed and the jet readjusted; the engine by now was suitably prepared for action. All this was very valuable tuition for us, and we were quick to ask the steam raisers and the following footplatemen all sorts of relevant questions. We were indeed preparing ourselves for our first firing trips.

As previously mentioned, it was 1939 and war with Germany was soon to be declared. With this in mind the Railway Company decided to quickly

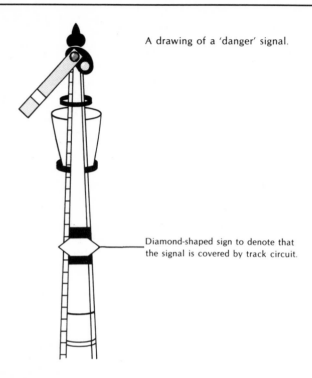

A drawing of a 'danger' signal.

Diamond-shaped sign to denote that
the signal is covered by track circuit.

promote cleaners to passed-cleaners. This meant that if a fireman failed to
turn up for duty or there were not enough firemen available, a passed-cleaner
would get the trip. If no trips were available, it was back to cleaning duties.

To progress from cleaners to passed-cleaners entailed correctly answering
a lot of questions, and proving to the examiner that a man was capable of
filling that position. The successful passed-cleaner must have a sound
knowledge of rules and regulations, and particularly be able to understand
Rule 55. This applied when an engine or train was stopped at a danger signal.
If this happened the fireman was required to go to the signal box and remind
the signalman about the position of his train. In the signalman's train book he
would insert the words 'Rule 55', the time of arrival at the signal box, and
clearly state which line they were standing on. He would also ask the
signalman to place a safety clip over the lever of the signal at which they were
standing. The railways have a first class safety system and this is just one
explanation of the efforts that are made to guarantee public safety.

If the signal in question had a diamond-shaped plate fixed to the signal post,
it was not always necessary for the fireman to leave his footplate. The driver
would give a long blast on his engine whistle and would assume that the signal
was track-circuited, and that a light would be showing in the signal box.
However, if there was any undue delay, most drivers would send their mates
to the signal box to ascertain just what was happening.

A fireman's duty was to ensure that on the tender were three long fire irons,
a shovel, a rake and a straight dart, the latter being available for knocking

clinker off the firebars. On preparation of his engine, he would obtain from the stores a full set of tools — these were carried in a bucket and consisted of a wooden handbrush, four spanners, a metal can with two red flags and twelve detonators safely secured inside. This can would be sealed with tape to ensure that the contents did not get damp or rusty. All the detonators needed to be examined to see if the fastening clips were intact. Detonators were a very essential part of the equipment that might have to be used to stop trains and, therefore, possibly save lives.

There would also be a paraffin lamp for the boiler gauge glass frame which should be filled and a good lampwick fitted inside. He would collect two engine headlamps, both fitted with red shades, and in good working order, also a firing shovel and coal pick. After depositing his tools on to the footplate, he would ensure that the engine smokebox door was tightly fastened, and the front and rear sand boxes would be filled with good riddled sand. The fire irons on the tender should be safely located on the rods provided. In the rack provided he would see that there were two boiler gauge glasses with fitments. There was a code of lamp positions for railway engines, denoting every type of train, and firemen and drivers should know them all. Usually, about 45 minutes to one hour was allowed for the fireman with his preparation duties and the same for the driver to oil and prepare his locomotive.

I ought to point out that drivers and firemen were expected to live in a certain radius of the engine sheds. This was to allow a caller-up, or knocker-up as they were sometimes called, to make sure that an engineman didn't overlay on night shifts. He would be called up in the daytime if it was found necessary. I was one of the unfortunates who had to leave home and find lodgings nearer to the engine sheds; my home was too far away. The black-out was in operation during these early years and it wasn't always pleasant turning out in the pitch darkness.

At that time, we fired for some of the older 'gentlemen' drivers. They had been brought up in the best railway tradition. They wore stiff white collars, and some even sported waxed moustaches, and they looked for all the world like the proverbial sergeant major. A lot of them had been brought up with the No. 1, 2 or 3 type freight locomotives. They were big men with little engines. I often felt that their followers were to become little men with big engines.

One of my first firing trips was on a local goods yard shunt engine, a Class 3 freight 0-6-0 tank type. The old driver I was with would probably retire about 1944. He was a very big man; in fact, he was so fat that he had to take off his overcoat to get through the handrails. I often helped to pull him into the engine cab or I am sure he would have got stuck.

With George we had to be on our mettle, only raise full steam when required, and not let the engine blow off at the safety valves. All this was to be good experience for the future. I must say this for my old mate — he did show me how not to stop an engine when shunting wagons in the sidings. If the engine brake was applied too quickly, the couplings on the wagons could break, so the message was clear, when shunting, before applying the brake, allow the wagons to stretch out and then they would stop as one. We once had an old Caledonian 0-6-0 tank engine on the same shunt job; heaven knows how that arrived at Hasland, but we were pleased to see it go. My old mate could not cope with it at all, he much preferred the Midland tanks.

Near the goods yard at Chesterfield is Horns Bridge, and during the war it

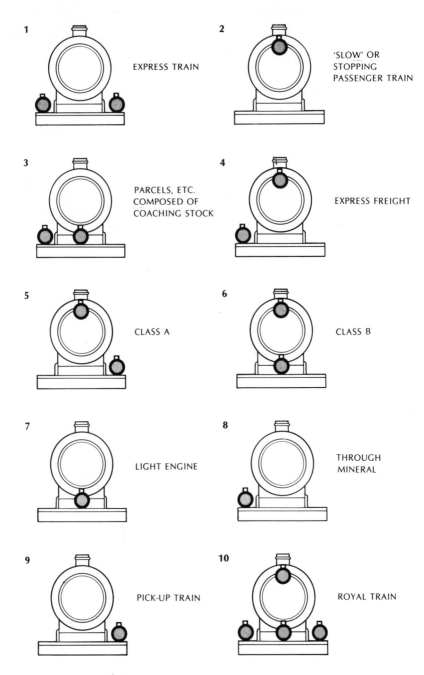

1 EXPRESS TRAIN

2 'SLOW' OR STOPPING PASSENGER TRAIN

3 PARCELS, ETC. COMPOSED OF COACHING STOCK

4 EXPRESS FREIGHT

5 CLASS A

6 CLASS B

7 LIGHT ENGINE

8 THROUGH MINERAL

9 PICK-UP TRAIN

10 ROYAL TRAIN

A brief description of the codes for engine headlamps.

was guarded by soldiers. This was a busy and important junction and the Germans must have listed it as one of their prime targets for air attack. Apart from two major roads it was at this point that three railway company lines criss-crossed; The Great Northern, Midland and Great Central lines. One night, we were walking to Chesterfield from Hasland, down the line to take over a train. Suddenly a voice barked, 'halt, who goes there'? We both stopped and wondered what the dickens was happening. I felt that these things only happen at the cinema. We had not been told about the sentries and this was our first encounter. After some embarrassing hesitation my mate shouted 'friend' and heard the crisp command 'come forward friend and be recognised — steady — just one at a time'. The soldier, standing with fixed bayonet and surrounded by thick gloom, looked as if he wasn't the type to stand for any nonsense. We each, in turn, had to produce our identification cards and then were told, 'pass friend'. This was truly a remarkable experience.

Most of the earlier trips involved firing on Class 3 or Class 4 freight engines and then on Class 2 passenger locomotives. Later on, we fired on almost every class of engine that one can mention, even the American locomotives that were sent over during the war.

Firing engines in the early days wasn't always easy. At Hasland, we had a lot of Class 4 freight types and each had its own character. Some liked heavy firing, others light, but all had to follow the basic principle for firing a Class 4 freight — that is a sloping fire. This means a heap of fire directly under the fire hole door, sloping to a low level under the brick arch. The brick arch was at the front end of the firebox and protected the tube ends from direct contact with the fire — it also aided combustion. When firing, it was always an advantage to break coal up in advance to lumps about as big as a man's fist. It was often an advantage to open the damper one notch with a Class 4 freight engine. This kept the sloping fire more intact; too much air from the damper often tended to rip the fire about. It was imperative for a fireman to keep the fire hole door open as little as possible so stopping cold air bringing down the firebox temperature. In almost all of the firebox openings there was a small flap. It was an aid to successful firing to fire 'over' that flap, again restricting airflow. In other type doors, with the latch for top and bottom, the same advantage was gained by firing over the bottom door.

All of this, of course, took time and experience. It was difficult enough in the early stages to fire engines when they were standing, but at speed it could be a nightmare. Drivers would grumble if a fireman 'littered' the footplate with coal.

One of the worst hazards for a beginner was that some engines were right-handed and some were left-handed. This meant that the driver could be seated at either the left or right side of the engine cab when working his controls. Most drivers objected to firemen using the wrong side of the cab when shovelling coal into the firebox, and as I am naturally right-handed I suffered this humiliation in the early days. However, after a lot of practice it was as easy to fire left-handed as right.

The larger engines, 8Fs, 9Fs, 'Black Fives' and 'Jubilees' and lots more, were all left-hand firing types. It's laughable now, but in the early years I actually used to hide firing shovels. If I came across a nice short lightweight shovel, I would try to hang on to it. At that time a lot of trips would bring us back to our home depots so that is where most of my hiding places were. Then, of

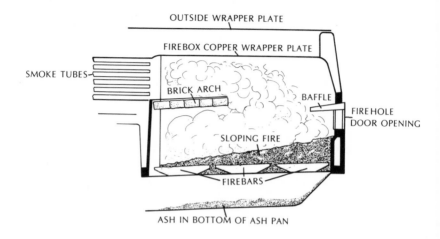

OUTSIDE WRAPPER PLATE

FIREBOX COPPER WRAPPER PLATE

SMOKE TUBES

BRICK ARCH

BAFFLE

FIREHOLE DOOR OPENING

SLOPING FIRE

FIREBARS

ASH IN BOTTOM OF ASH PAN

A side view sketch of a firebox.

course, the opposite would happen, and we would be relieved by another crew or change over engines. So you see, my stock of hidden shovels could not last for ever. Sometimes, careless firemen on preparation duties would put damaged shovels aboard, but mostly they had more sense. It did happen that when a fireman noticed a shovel that was not to his liking, he would swap it with a shovel from another engine footplate. I must confess that I have done this, but mainly to get a longer handled shovel. These were much better and saved a fireman from burning his hands. They were also a great help in getting coal into the back corners of the firebox; that was where the majority of engines liked it most. By looking into the box when firing operations were in progress, the old engines would almost tell you where they wanted their feed of coal. If a really bright spot could be seen, bang some coal on it — that was the order of the day. It was often noticeable with Class 4 freights that a fireman could keep a not too good steamer around the 140 mark on the steam pressure gauge, the maximum blowing off for this engine being 175lb. We have gone miles in these situations and not until the driver has eased off with his regulator has the steam pressure risen. To sit on any steam engine at speed and hear the safety-valves occasionally 'pop off' was a fireman's delight. This was obviously appreciated by the driver who would no doubt nudge the engine along a bit faster. It was all a matter of team-work really. If a shovelful of coal into the firebox was followed by a puff of smoke, a fireman was, more or less, achieving his objective. Equally, if there was a lot of thick black smoke, proper combustion was not always taking place. There was then too much unburnt coal in the box.

The chimney was often a good tell-tale as to how and when to fire an engine. Every fireman would have his own method. It wasn't a bad idea to take a bit of advice from crewmen who had a lot of experience. Most of us at Hasland knew which of our own engines were good or bad steamers. With this knowledge, we could take steps to assist in our efforts to maintain steam. If we knew we had a good steamer that would be fine, but if otherwise, we would make sure that the smokebox door was securely fastened. If we didn't have decent coal on the tender, sometimes we might tip a load of decent coal on the back, if the tender would hold it. We would look at the tube ends inside the firebox just over the brick arch, and if these were furred up with scale, steps would be taken to remove this. In all engine sheds there were long steel rods with a flat plate attached to the end. These were on racks on the shed walls. They were called tube plate scrapers and we could remove a lot of the offending scale by this method. A nice clean tube plate was certainly an advantage to a good steaming performance.

A trick some enginemen used, was to wait until they left the depot, select a place where they could have a good clear run, remove the baffle plate, and after the driver had fully opened the regulator with the lever down, the fireman would throw a shovelful of sand at the tube plate ends. Then there would be smoke and dust for everybody, which would come belting out of the chimney. Hard lines for anyone in that area who had their clean washing hung out to dry. The authorities would have frowned at this practice, but it could be very effective.

Another method used by enginemen to help an engine steam more freely was to place a 'jimmy' across the top of the blast pipe. This would help to sharpen the blast; the fireman would probably have to work a bit harder but with better results. 'Jimmy' was a local nickname to describe a bolt or piece of steel bar. A favourite method was to remove the handle from our bucket, straighten the hooks at each end, and fit the pointed ends into the holes of the blower-pipe ring, then securely fasten the rod down with a piece of strong wire. It would be interesting to see a collection of these, as they came in all shapes and sizes. It was quite an operation fitting them into the top of the blast pipe, care being taken that they were placed 'dead centre'. This was a dangerous practice as these objects could have fallen down the blast pipe and done a lot of damage.

Once on a firing trip with a Class 4 freight, my driver told me that he had 'jimmied' our engine. She was reputed to be a bad steamer. Halfway on our journey my mate informed me that we would be swapping over footplates with another crew and returning home. Stopping at a danger signal he requested me to go to the smokebox, open the door and remove his treasured bucket handle. This I did, the signal turned to green and off we went. Unfortunately, we did not change over and had to go the full journey with the Class 4. She behaved perfectly, so perhaps that was one occasion when the previously mentioned practice wasn't necessary.

We learned a lot of tricks as firemen, everyday appeared to be different — changeable weather conditions, dealing with bad steamers, derailments, engines slipping — all sorts of things were happening and had to be dealt with.

A nice little tip from an older fireman was this. When firing a No. 8 freight, 'Black Five', 'Jubilee', 5XP or any of the longer firebox type of engine, always keep a good lot of coal at the back of the firebox, just under the fire hole door. Keep this heap to about a yard or so long and then, when delivering coal into the firebox, bounce the shovel off this heap. The shovel would then, in fact, be well inside the fire. A simple tip, but very effective. The long firebox appeared to be much shorter when using this method. Less experienced firemen had a tendency to throw coal only as far as the middle section, and this prevented any more coal from reaching the front end. The result would then be a loss of steam. The only thing that could be done to rectify this was for the fireman to get the long rake from the tender and push the obstruction forward. Too much raking would tend to make the fire run on to the firebars, and so create clinker.

A lot of passenger work at Hasland involved assisting express trains to Leeds. If the train engine crew were struggling to maintain steam, or their train was overloaded, permission would be given for an assisting engine. We mainly had the No. 2 passenger 4-4-0 type of locomotive and we coupled up to trains at either Hasland or Chesterfield. After our run to Leeds, we would turn our engine and be ready to assist trains travelling south.

On a similar trip to Leeds things turned out to be very different. We coupled up to an express at Chesterfield and my mate had to give our engine second regulator right up the bank to Bradway Tunnel. The rear engine didn't appear to be pulling many trees up. Leaving Sheffield we passed on to Rotherham, Swinton, Wath and on to Cudworth, and looking back at the rear engine, I was amazed to see that the driver had shut down steam. No wonder my mate was being so heavy with the controls. We raced down to Normanton and on to the dead end station at Leeds. Getting off our engine to uncouple, I saw the fireman of the train engine standing on the platform — he was as black as a coal miner. In his cockney accent he told me about their trip from London.

There had been a lot of bombing around the St. Pancras area and he had managed with very little sleep. He was worried about leaving his family, as it would be the following day before he returned home. The London crew were required to lodge at Leeds. 'That is bad enough', he exclaimed, 'but the engine has really caused us some trouble today'. Parts of the brick arch had been continually falling into the firebox. Then, when they were leaving Sheffield Station, the whole lot of fire bricks had fallen down — that explained why we had been working so hard. Our No. 2 passenger engine had been hauling a dead engine and a load of coaches. The cockneys would leave their engine on the ash pit at Holbeck Shed, and whoever had to clean out that firebox would find it heavy work shovelling the large bricks out into the ash pit.

I was once asked what coal consisted of and confessed that I did not know. Then I was given a little tip. Always try to remember two words — these were 'NO CASH', and this was the answer. Taking the letters in those two words we have Nitrogen, Oxygen, Carbon, Ash, Sulphur and Hydrogen.

During the war years, engines were often neglected, and there were many reasons for this; fitters being called into the forces before the essential works order was applied, engines expected to do more than their fair share before being boiler washed or properly repaired, quick turn rounds from other depots, resulting in engines being away from parent depots for weeks on end. The black-out didn't help; these were not ideal conditions for fitters to work in anyway. On their journeys, drivers often had difficulty seeing signals, their vision impaired by steam escaping from cylinder glands, valve spindles and numerous other parts of their engines. Maintaining steam could be a nightmare because of the waste just mentioned. Drivers and fireman had to be on their mettle, taking into account the varying types of coal which were available at that time. Sometimes Welsh coal was on the engine tenders; this seemed to stick on to the firebars, clinkering early. Firemen would use the long steel straight dart to break the clinker up and so allow air from the ash pan to reach under the fire. With their rakes they could lift large lumps of clinker up from under the fire hole door section of the bars in the same way. Often they would do this when 'on the road' and, after first putting the clinker on the steel footplate to cool down, would kick it out on to the permanent way. If trains were standing at signals, one could often see firemen doing a quick fire-cleaning operation. The platelayers didn't like these heaps of clinker piling up along their neat track. However, whenever it was possible we would use our shovels and spread the clinker and ash along the railside ballast.

It was a joy to have Grimethorpe 'hard' coal on the tender; this was usually in clean hard lumps. A quick tap down the grain of the coal with our coal pick and the coal easily split. This was very clean and after using it on long journeys, engines have returned to base with the fire almost as clean as when they set off. The engine disposing crews had only to riddle fire ash through the gaps in the firebars to clean the fire. Another time they would have to take an engine on to the ash pit if it had been using opencast coal. This could be very clean or sometimes just the opposite. We noticed that fireboxes were very deep in ash after using that 'stuff'.

Some funny experiences were had with coal on the ex-L&YR engines. This was of a queer variety and seemed to run on to the firebars almost like treacle. I was never very fussy with 'Lankie' engines and, at the best of times, when firing with this particular type of coal, didn't relish it one bit. A good way of helping to avoid clinkering was as follows. Before starting on a journey and when the fire was clean, get some pieces of fire brick, break them up and carefully strew them along over the firebars. This had a tendency to hold the clinker off the bars and so allow better air flow under the fire from the damper, and there was the added advantage that when finally disposing of the engine and cleaning the fire, the clinker would be easier to knock off the bars with the straight dart. A little heavier to throw out, of course, but well worth the initial effort.

Some engines had drop grates, and others had rocker grates; these could be operated from the engine cab by using a long steel bar handle. A fireman could rock the firebars en route, so allowing loose ash to fall into the ash pan. It was also possible to liberate clinker in this way. The trouble was that if a fireman became too ambitious in his fire-cleaning duties, he could be in for a load of trouble. If a large, hard, piece of clinker fell through, it could become wedged, and that was where the problems started. If they were lucky they could liberate these obstructions with the aid of the rake of the dart, and most drivers would cast a wary eye on their mates, and try to ensure that they didn't get too carried away.

Another danger, of course, in rocking the bars on a journey, was that fire could inadvertantly fall into the ash pan. With the engine in motion and the rush of air under the locomotive, the ash pan could easily get very hot and consequently buckle in or be damaged. There was a period when wood was tipped on to engine tenders; crews would try to avoid having too much of this as it would be almost impossible to maintain steam with wood alone. Pictures are shown on television where the stokers are throwing logs into the big Canadian locomotives. On a recent film about small railways of the world, the engines seemed to burn anything. The wood that I am referring to on British engines was of the bark type. They were odd-shaped pieces and tended to stick

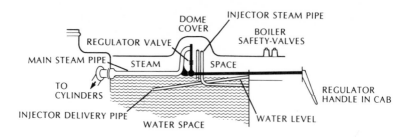

Engines would prime if water got into these pipes and connections.

The highest point of the steam space above water level was in the dome. Steam there was driest, hence the positioning of the regulator valve, steam pipes to injectors, etc. On the taper boiler engines the auxiliary fittings were supplied with steam from a steam manifold, mounted on the back of the firebox.

A sketch of a dome-type engine.

up in the firebox; this could easily cause holes in the fire, too much air would rush in and the temperature would fall. So, with this in mind, it was a good idea to try and get a good coal fire burning and then deposit the wood amongst it. We used to stack the wood on to the footplate as it fell down from the tender hole, sometimes even putting pieces on to the food box top, then when the fire was really incandescent, try to emulate Casey Jones and bowl the logs inside. One of the worst set-backs to a driver and fireman having a good trip was engine 'priming'. This was when the boilers became too full and water got into the pipes which were situated in the 'dome'; they were placed at this high point to collect dry steam. Usually, when engines did prime, it was because firemen were a little nervous and wanted to get a good start. They sometimes got a bit fidgety, and when the water level showed in the boiler gauge glass, they just had to fill the boiler up again. They didn't seem to grasp the idea that when the driver eventually opened the regulator the water would 'lift'. After heavy sessions of priming, cylinder gland packing could be damaged, water being allowed to get into the brake pipes causing the train to slow down. It seemed ages before the engines really dried out and got over their 'sickness'.

To fully illustrate this point here is a little incident that once happened at Chesterfield Station.

The famous *Flying Scotsman* was paying a visit to Chesterfield. It looked beautiful in its livery of shining green, and people had travelled from miles around to see her, and children were ecstatic. A young local fireman who was 'train mad' was on the footplate of the *Flying Scotsman*. It was his day off and he had 'tagged on' with the engine crew whilst they were having this short stay in town. All the brass hats were around and, at times, the footplate on the large engine seemed to be crowded with people. The young fireman was anxious to show everyone that he could stoke-up engines and, when room was available, started to shovel coal into the firebox. Unfortunately, he was being carried away by the atmosphere of this famous occasion, and he just kept on throwing coal into the box. The train was not due to leave Chesterfield Station for another hour, and gradually the huge fire started to get hold. Steam rose and the engine safety-valves lifted; the noise was deafening. The fireman kept putting on the injector, then things were quietened down for a while and the inevitable happened. The boiler became too full; no longer could they keep quietening the engine down and she blew off continuously. There were a lot of red faces and the driver and fireman must have felt relieved when it was finally time to depart. Sadly the damage had been done, the engine boiler was still much too full. The guard waved his green flag and the *Flying Scotsman* left the station on its journey south. She was far from flying, in fact you could almost say she was crying, and water was belching out of her chimney. People were lining the banks and sidings at the lineside; they couldn't hear themselves speak above the din. Instead of the sight of a gracious departure, we were witnessing the sight of a beautiful locomotive being bogged down by too much water inside her boiler — she must have really felt sick. The driver had the cylinder cocks wide open and the train was only crawling out of the station. Instances like this were added proof that priming was a nuisance. Engine boilers were washed out at intervals and hopefully scum and dirt removed; there was a time when drivers carried tins of powder to mix with the water in the tender tank, but I cannot recollect what the powder contained, even though it was supposed to help soften the water and help to minimise priming.

Talking about leaking glands reminds me of one of my old mates. He used to place his mashing can full of tea on the small dish plate, which was just over the fire hole door — like a mantlepiece if you like. When the regulator gland started to leak it would often allow water to run out all over the can lid. The old driver seemed oblivious of this and just kept drinking the stuff. I am sure that he would never have trouble priming. Heaven knows how much of that boiler powder he must have consumed. I swear that the tea often looked green and it's a wonder it didn't make the old lad sick. He once did have a spate of boils on his neck — I wonder if this had caused it. The chap reached a ripe old age so it obviously didn't do him any real bodily harm.

Once when firing for this same driver, we had been on the footplate for long hours, were standing with our engine at Chinley Station and were to follow the local passenger train. We were both very hungry, rationing was still on, and food coupons were required for people to obtain most of the eat-able things. The old driver asked me to nip up to the local little shop and see if I might be able to buy some food. The only thing the shopkeeper would allow me to purchase were a few vanilla sandwiches. Triumphantly, I returned with these to our footplate. My mate was disgusted and soon went to great lengths to tell me that men could not work engines on 'puff pastry'. Come to think about it, there isn't much nourishment in them is there?

This same driver was one of the best men that I ever fired for. He was generous in his work sharing. He would drive the engine one day and allow me to drive the next. It didn't matter what type of train turned up, if it was my turn to drive, I would be put in the driver's seat. This meant that I was able to get a good knowledge of driving goods trains, passenger trains, the lot.

Not long ago, I read in a newspaper that the giant carbonisation plant at

Wingerworth was celebrating its 25th anniversary. This is a vast complex and stretches for miles. A driver once allowed me to work a train into the 'up' sidings for this particular plant. We had picked up our wagons at Seymour, and these consisted of about 20 loads of coal next to our tender, then some empty chemical tanks, and the rear section, again, consisted of coal wagons. When going into the sidings with this train, we looked back and were amazed to see the tank wagons jumping all over the place. The engine was brought to a standstill gently, but the weight at the rear end helped to pile the tank wagons up into the air. It was a spectacular sight and we were relieved to learn that the lines had moved and that we were not responsible for the serious derailment. The lines and sleepers had been laid on loose ballast, and after a heavy rainfall this had become worse, and our train suffered the consequences. There was a lot of subsidence in our area, particularly between Chesterfield and Leeds or York, via the old route. These were colliery districts so these things were expected to happen.

Remember the old saying 'a policeman's lot is not a happy one'. Believe me, at times a railwayman's wasn't either. If he was married he would need to have an understanding wife, and if he was courting — heaven help him. Many a courtship must have been broken by the inconvenience of the then existing shift system. You could not expect a girl to wait forever.

After the initial long term system with the same mate, our depot introduced a 12 week system. We had 12 links consisting of 12 jobs. That was 144 different turns of duty. Coupled to this, if a man was 'passed' he had the added humbug of being subject to requirements. A passed-cleaner might turn up for shed cleaning duties and go out firing; a passed-fireman could turn up for his booked firing job and go out driving. There was always the possibility of a footplateman becoming ill, or on holiday, and he had to be covered. Similarly, most depots had an engine on stand-by; after all, engines could be ill you know, they might even have a breakdown.

In later years, when the diesels were on trial, a steam engine stand-by was always the order of the day at all depots. It was an advantage for a passed-fireman to have a knowledge of as many routes as possible; greater then were his chances of being called out and getting his trips in. If he knew the local passenger stations it was an added advantage. Some of these stations took a bit of learning. Take Sheffield (Midland) for example. There were about 90 signals in that one station and all had to be learned. A lot of them might only be the dolly type, but pass one at danger and a driver could be in trouble, perhaps even derailing his locomotive. If this happened he would have some explaining to do, and may even end up being suspended from duty, or even be requested to have another eyesight test.

Here is a little trick that was used when an engine became derailed, and it always sticks in my mind.

A small 0-6-0 tank engine became derailed, and another engine was backing up to try to pull the derailed engine back on the rails. Timber was packed under the flanges of the derailed engine's wheels, but when the buffers of the two engines were touching, they were at a sharp angle. The couplings would not, therefore, meet, and as there was no strong chain available, quick thinking prevailed; one of the drivers unscrewed both couplings to their full length, and turned them to the vertical position, he then inserted a fishplate in the last link of each engine coupling — the end result — one long coupling. Both drivers opened up their engine regulators and the tank engine got back on to the 'right lines'. A quick check would be made on axleboxes, brasses, springs, etc., and if these were all right, the engine would be ready for work again.

We were once on a derailed locomotive but were not so lucky to get her back on to the rails. The rail broke in two or three places and our shunt engine turned over on to its side. It finished up on a level crossing, and the bottom step on the fireman's side dug into a sleeper; but for that, the engine would have landed completely on its side. My mate bailed out and I was left staring into the sky. I was a bit shaken but none the worse for my experience.

The war was really on by now and the lads at the depot joined the Home Guard. We elected one of the fitters to be our Officer, a guard was the sergeant, somebody else was corporal, and the rest of us — well, it was so embarrassing. We paraded like true soldiers, but had brush stakes instead of rifles. We practiced mock attacks, but, thank goodness, we were not called upon to defend ourselves with such weapons. Mind you, if 'Jerry' had been confronted with us and our primitive weapons he might just have collapsed with sheer surprise. Some of the brawnier firemen had shovels over their shoulders, so perhaps they might have looked more fearsome, and frightened 'Jerry' away. One thing is certain — whatever the odds — the lads would have fought hard for their families.

By now we were firing regularly and were promoted to firemen, no more engine cleaning, or engine shed duties. The more firing trips we got, the higher our wages would become. There was a passenger link, lodging link, goods, colliery trips, shunters and engine shed disposing, and preparation links. At the depot were Class 4 freights, 8Fs, Beyer-Garratts, tank engines, and lots of other different types of locomotive. On the local passenger trips our faithful No. 2 passenger 4-4-0 type was regularly used; an ideal type of train for this engine would be about five coaches, approximately 155 tons. They were mostly free steaming engines and caused few problems in that direction. The worst hazard was slipping, this being due to their large 7ft. 6in. driving wheels not adhering to the rails. To appreciate the function of these high wheels, one had to be travelling on a good long level section of track.

Drivers tried to ensure that the sanders were always working properly, taking care that there were no pebbles mixed into the sand that would cause blockages in the sand traps. In all the engine sheds were sand houses. These were usually separate brick-built buildings which housed a brick-type kiln with a fire, bricked all around. Sand was riddled and placed in a large oven which was over the fire. After the sand was thoroughly dried, it was ready for use in the engine sand boxes. Sometimes, carelessness prevailed and the sand was not riddled. This is where trouble could start because pebbles would foul the apparatus. Drivers often carried a strong piece of wire to remove these obstructions. Removing the bottom cork they could poke around and sometimes were able to dislodge the pebbles. If it was possible, and the engine was standing, a driver could remove the cover from the sand trap and get at the pebbles more easily.

We used to work passenger trains to Barnsley. The station was situated on top of a gradient and we often had slipping sessions when approaching it. I cannot recommend the practice, as it was very dangerous, but we have sometimes removed the bottom cork on the sanders, filled the firing shovel with sand and, walked in front of a slipping locomotive, sprinkling sand on to

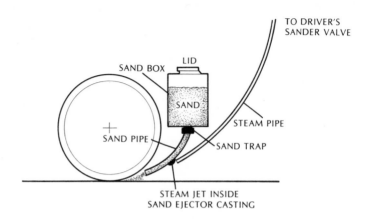

When steam was admitted to the base of the sand pipe, it created a partial vacuum inside the pipe. Air was induced to enter under the hood of the sand trap at the base of the sand box. This air lifted a layer of sand, and carried it into the sand pipe. The same jet of steam which was used in the first place would carry sand with force right under the engine's driving wheels. By a flick of the handle on the footplate, a driver could control either front or rear sanders. This was an advantage when travelling tender first.

On many small tank engines used in collieries, etc., simple or dry sanders were used. These incorporated a handle and connections direct to the base of the sand box. Obviously, these would soon run empty if left open too long.

A sketch of a steam sander.

the rails. Standing on the framing steps we would take sand from the top of the sand box and repeat the operation. With the constantly slipping wheels and slashing about of the side rods, it was really a stupid thing to do, but at the time it seemed a lot better than bringing the train to a standstill. On the same run we once had Tilbury, 4-4-2 No. 3 passenger type tank engines. They had some at Toton and we had two of them at Hasland. We called them 'crooners' and were a bit afraid of them, mainly because we didn't understand the working of the boiler water injectors. They were, to us, so unreliable, but we had to adapt and try to put up with them.

One day, again on the Sheffield to Barnsley run with a 'crooner', the boiler safety-valves stuck wide open. In all my railway career this was the only time I saw this happen. We were approaching Chapeltown and the noise was deafening. The driver asked permission to uncouple the old 'crooner', then he tried rushing forward and stopping quickly, he jumped the wheels off some fishplates, but all to no avail, so we exchanged engines with one that was standing in the sidings. It was a No. 3 freight type engine but we accepted it to get us to Barnsley. Luckily there was a passenger engine available in Barnsley Station so we again swapped engines. When we watched our old 'crooner' being taken to Grimethorpe engine shed, she was really 'crooning' her head off. Again we were all pleased to see the back of those Tilbury engines, but no doubt locomen who were used to them would not agree with us.

Referring again to our own No. 2 passenger engines reminds me of the earlier days. Drivers sometimes had their own engines or, more correctly, engines booked down to them. The crews took great pride in their 'charges', polishing the brasswork, vaselining the black boiler front, rubbing tallow on the yellow cab roof and polishing the windows, etc. They even used a stick and emery paper to make patterns on the gleaming regulator handle. It was truly a locoman's delight, and it's a pity photographs are not available to really illustrate what I mean. At that time, we had a trip which took us to York, then to Wakefield, back to York, then express work south. There was a stretch of line on the North Eastern Railway where their trains came down an incline from the Leeds direction. The fast and slow lines then ran parallel almost to York where two trains were timed to meet at the same time. It was an expected thing for the Midland crews to watch for this train, and when they came almost side by side, try to race them.

Passengers also seemed to enjoy this bit of rivalry but, sad to say, the North Eastern lads nearly always beat us; perhaps they had more powerful engines, or that downhill bit helped them along. The race couldn't last long as both trains would soon be approaching York Station, and one would have to make way and eventually follow the other. Sitting high up in their bucket seats the 'foreigners' would be like cats with cream, making sure they were first into York.

During the war, and with the black-out laws being in operation, all locomotives were required to carry tarpaulin sheets; for the cab type, a small sheet to fit from tender to cab top, then side windows blackened. The other classes would have both a top sheet and one for each side. These were obviously to try and avoid firebox glare whenever the fire hole doors had to be opened. If the air raid warning had been given, engine crews would try to ensure that no light could be seen by enemy aircraft. Firemen would be encouraged to be quick in their firing duties, but the dilemma was that as coal was shovelled from a full tender, gaps would appear and the light from the firebox shone out almost like a searchlight. On warmer evenings it could be really stuffy firing in these conditions. When firing was complete, the sheets would be hastily drawn to one side so that fresh air could enter the cab.

Looking back, I feel that most trains must have been easily seen from the air — black-out sheets or not. The very fact that they were steam engines was too hard to disguise, as smoke, steam and general movement must have been pretty obvious. However, precautions had to be taken as trains did pass through towns, villages, industrial areas and the like. It would have caused quite a commotion if an ammunition train had been blown up passing through a busy populated area.

Most things were rationed during the war as goods were in short supply. People learned to pull out all the stops and used their wits to survive. A thing that might interest ladies was this — nylon stockings were almost unobtainable. My girlfriend, like many others, used to rub wet sand all over her legs, she would then let it dry, and then gently rub it off — result, nice sandy coloured legs. To get the perfect result they would then ask someone to draw nice straight lines down the back — this was to simulate the stocking seams.

The Government used to tell us to eat carrots as these were good for our eyes — fighter pilots were supposed to be encouraged to eat them so that they could see better in the dark. I never noticed any improvement in my eyes after eating carrots, and when working on engines with steam leaking all around them, we would almost need binoculars to see where we were going.

Eggs, too, were practically non-existent, and we were allocated rations of egg powder. This stuff smelt rather vile, but was alright when used for cooking omelettes, etc. One day one of our cleaners was grumbling about his sandwiches. 'I've got some of that new fangled egg powder for lunch', he told us. He certainly had, his lunch tin consisted of bread and butter with the wretched stuff, in powder form, spread all over it. His mother had certainly not read the cooking instructions on the packet, and would feel very embarrassed when her son brought home his uneaten sandwiches and said, 'Here mum, smell that lot'.

A lady at Ilkeston learned the art of survival in good time. We were passing her home and on the railings were rows of empty bottles. They resembled a coconut shy, and we could not resist throwing at them. Selecting suitable pieces of coal from the tender we had a bit of target practice. This happened on one or two occasions, and one day we noticed the lady raking the coal from under the fence; that's enterprise for you, I bet her coal house was never empty.

Chapter Two

THE SHEFFIELD BLITZ

After about four months of war, things were really beginning to happen on the railways. Already sections of line had been damaged and we were all put on full alert. One just didn't know what the next day might bring. The 'Luftwaffe' had repeatedly bombed London and had inflicted tremendous damage to our capital city. Thousands of people were made homeless and many lives were lost. In spite of this, the civil defence, police, Army, and those civilians lucky enough to still be alive, all played their part in bringing sanity back on to the streets. The German High Command was obviously aware of this and, for a change, turned its attention to the possible destruction of other cities.

I will never forget the time when the 'Jerries' decided to bomb Sheffield. It was a Thursday evening, 12th December 1940, and we had signed on duty at Hasland Shed at about 6.30p.m. We were on relief duty and the Control would select a train for us to 'relieve'. The sirens in Chesterfield had already sounded that night, and their strange alarming sounds sent a sense of fear through all of us who heard them. We were on air raid warning 'red' — enemy planes had already crossed the coast and were heading inland. Over in the direction of Sheffield the searchlights were tentatively probing the skies. It was a beautiful clear, but cold, night, with a full moon, and the stars were clearly visible in the skies. It wasn't long before we could hear the strange, by now familiar, throb of enemy aircraft. They seemed to be coming over the far side of Chesterfield in waves. In the distance the Sheffield anti-aircraft guns were opening up, and soon all hell was let loose. Arriving over the city, enemy planes were diving down out of the night skies, and the first batch were dropping flares and incendiary bombs. Other planes were shooting down those huge clumsy barrage balloons that had surrounded Sheffield since the beginning of the war. These were supposed to bring down low flying aircraft but the 'Luftwaffe' were making sure that this did not happen to any of their planes. People were already trying to put out the fires caused by the incendiary devices, but the German aircraft gunners were machine-gunning pedestrians at will. This was the sort of night that the enemy was to revel in. They not only had their flares, incendiaries and bombs for guidance, but the moon was on their side too. In those conditions one wondered just how they could fail to hit their intended targets.

By the side of the railway line at Hasland we were helpless spectators, witnessing this awesome spectacle and the possible destruction of our neighbouring city.

Suddenly, we were jolted to our senses by the ringing of the telephone in the relief cabin close by. It was the Controller and he was about to instruct us to relieve the crew of the 'Scotsman' — the Midland's version of the London to Glasgow express train. My heart leapt, this was to be my first trip on a big engine on an express passenger train, and I had never envisaged that my baptism was to be in such frightening circumstances. What would we be heading for? Could we possibly be lucky enough to take a train right through the centre of Sheffield and come out of it unscathed? Again the phone rang, and this time it was the signalman calling from Hasland signal box to tell us that our train was now approaching on the 'down' main line. Picking up our haversacks and mashing cans, we walked nervously towards the signal box. The giant locomotive was moving slowly towards us, as if it knew that something was wrong. Passengers were sticking their heads out of the open windows and dozens of faces were peering up into the sky.

We relieved the Millhouses men on the footplate, and after they had informed us that we had ten coaches to the rear, and that the weight would be approximately 330 tons, the Sheffield men disembarked to let themselves into the first coach. My mate gave them a hurried report of what was happening ahead and they were obviously already very concerned about the safety of their families. I will always remember our engine that night, it was a Class 4-6-0 'Jubilee', No. 5627 *Sierra Leone*. The 'down' main line starting signal was lowered and we moved off in the direction of Horns Bridge and Chesterfield, making sure that the side and top tarpaulins were firmly in position, preparing to show as little light from the fire to the enemy as possible.

When we approached Tapton Junction, the signalman diverted us on to the old route to Sheffield, via Barrow Hill and Eckington. Stopping us at his signal box he informed my mate and the train guard that the control had requested the diversion and dared not risk the train into Sheffield Station under these conditions.

As we set off in the direction of Whittington, we could see to our left the skies over Sheffield getting even brighter. Even though we were ten or twelve miles away, the ground seemed to be shaking around us. People at Barrow Hill engine shed, and the huge Staveley Works complex, must have wondered if they too were to get a taste of the Germans' fury.

We didn't know then, but were later to learn that rows and rows of houses in Sheffield were being destroyed, large departmental stores gutted, and trams were burning in the streets. There is no doubt that before the raid first started, people would have been filling the local pubs and cinemas. A lot of these poor unfortunate Yorkshire folk would seek shelter in the basements of the big shops and stores, others taking to the public house cellars. Some were to be buried alive under the rubble after the large buildings came crashing down upon them. The raid was to last about nine hours and, no doubt, the Germans would be thinking that they had destroyed a vital part of one of the country's biggest armaments producers. The fact is that it was the city centre that suffered the worst hit. This was certainly an unforgettable experience for us and, as we continued on our way towards Eckington and Killamarsh, we couldn't help counting our blessings.

Passing Canklow Sheds we noticed the groups of people gathered around, no doubt praying that the raid would soon be over and that they would be spared by any stray raider. We were soon at Rotherham (Masboro') Station and our Sheffield passengers alighted. They would probably have to make their way home by other means, as surely no trains would be allowed to go from Rotherham, via Brightside, to Sheffield. It is sad to say that for some people 'home' would no doubt be only just a memory.

The journey from Chesterfield to Rotherham with *Sierra Leone* was no real challenge from a fireman's point of view, as this was virtually a downhill section of line. However, as I mentioned earlier, this was only my first trip on a big locomotive, and I was soon made aware that throwing coal to the front end of a long firebox was not that easy. My driver was the considerate type and was always ready to give me advice on just when to pick up the shovel. In fact, he occasionally picked it up himself, and showed me how the job should be done. As we went on our way up to Cudworth and Royston, then on to Normanton and Leeds, the engine was steaming quite freely. Thinking about what the people of Sheffield had endured on that fateful evening, overshadowed any other thoughts that I might have had about my maiden journey on an express passenger train. For those unfortunate people there was more to come and, sadly, on the Sunday evening, just three days afterwards, the 'Luftwaffe' struck again. This was a shorter but heavier attack, heavy bombs, land mines, the lot, were again thrown at Sheffield. The raid lasted from 7.00p.m. to 10.00p.m. on 15th December, and many parts of the city which had escaped the first raid suffered severe damage. More than 600 citizens lost their lives, many were missing, presumed dead, and thousands of houses were damaged or destroyed. At the height of the bombing, a driver and fireman from Hasland were among the unfortunates who happened to be on duty in Sheffield (Midland) Station. Bert was the fireman and he personally gave me his account of just what happened.

A bomb dropped very near to them as they sat on the footplate of their No. 2 passenger engine on Pond Street turntable. The blast lifted all the coal off the engine tender, the tank was punctured by shrapnel, water spurted out as from a colander. Bert said that he and his driver must have been hurled against the engine cab, possibly even the roof and they were semi-conscious, the driver sustaining damaged ribs. When they gained full consciousness but were still suffering from shock, they managed to get away from their crippled engine and seek some sort of protection under the short tunnel at the south end of the station. The station buildings suffered severe damage and lengths of track were destroyed. The old houses all around the Pond Street area were razed to the ground. It was to be a long time before the new city of Sheffield emerged, and a heavy price was paid on those nights.

Chapter Three

ACCIDENTS, COAL AND WATER

Back at the engine sheds one cold, rainy, and miserable, evening, locomotive crews were busy preparing and disposing engines. One of the drivers was in the act of coaling up engine duties, and his locomotive was standing under the coal hopper. They had already tipped two or three tubs of coal on to the tender, and then it happened! The driver was sending another tub up into the air when it came crashing down; the full weight would be about half a ton. He tried to dive out of the way, but the coal tub dropped across the unfortunate man's legs. Men were quickly on the scene and some of them held a tarpaulin over the injured driver to protect him from the pouring rain. Two other engine drivers lifted the tub off the driver's legs. He was bleeding badly and one driver stopped this by putting a thumb and finger on to a pressure point. Meanwhile, another driver administered the necessary first aid. Fortunately, both these men were St. John Ambulance trained men, and were later to receive the coveted gold medal for their prompt actions. The injured man was taken to hospital and, owing to the serious complications, was off work for a long time.

But let us recap on this short story — two men lifted a 10 cwt. iron coal tub from an injured driver's legs; it must have been the will of God that gave these chaps such strength. Many times after the accident they were asked how they did it, but strangely each time they tried they couldn't even budge a full coal tub.

We were constantly being told that at all times we must ensure that the fire irons were securely fastened on the engine tenders. To do this meant that we would locate the round handles of the three fire irons on to the tender safety bars. There were occasions when fire irons fell off tenders of engines travelling at speed, and some of these caused severe damage. Stories were told about long rakes, darts, or clinker shovels clattering across station platforms, some coming to 'rest' in station restaurant rooms. One can imagine how dangerous it would be if one of these fire irons came crashing through a window. Whenever I heard of this happening my thoughts always went back to a tragic incident involving a young mate of mine.

Albert had started work at Hasland on the same day as me and we both were promoted to passed-cleaners at the same time. One weekend he was the fireman on an Avenue Sidings to Birmingham coal train. They would take wagon loads of slack for the Midlands power-stations, lodge at the barracks at Saltley, and then return with an empty wagon train for the north. On the return journey they had passed through Clay Cross Station on the main line, then switched on to the goods line to proceed to Avenue Sidings. Albert must have looked into the firebox of their engine, realised that the fire inside was

Plate 1: Midland Railway Kirtley 0-6-0, No. 1961 at Hasland Shed, spotlessly clean and decorated with flowers, ready to take part in Queen Victoria's visit to Sheffield. The coal on the tender back certainly looks hand picked!

B. Handford

Plate 2: At the controls of a Class 1P 4-4-0 engine in the 1920s. Hasland driver A. Whelan and his fireman W. Marchant. This driver retired in 1937.

A. Whelan

Plate 3: An LMS period photograph of an 0-6-0 tank engine backing into Chesterfield Goods Yard with a train of pulp for the nearby Robinsons Brampton Works. No. 7112 has certainly got a heavy load on and the works directors are on the scene to check their urgent material. To the left is the Brampton branch line where the wagons would eventually have been taken.

Alec Robinson

Plate 4: Horns Bridge circa 1905. This view clearly shows why 'Jerry' would want this on his target list during the war time bombing raids over England. It was a place where 3 Railway Companies converged. Lancashire and East Coast Railways at the top; London Midland in the centre, and the Great Central 'up' and 'down' lines below.

Courtesy of Chesterfield Library

Plate 5: No. 43433, Class 3F, with a long load of empty wagons approaching Tapton Junction on the 'down' goods line, on 28 August 1954.

B. Goodlad

Plate 6: A Hasland (18C) engine, No. 491, one of my favourite class 2P 4-4-0 types, hauls a slow passenger train into Dore & Totley Station on the 'up' main line, prior to nationalisation.

P. Hughes

Plate 7: No. 44267, Class 4F, locomotive returning empty holiday coaches to Millhouses carriage sidings on 16 July 1955.

B. Goodlad

Plate 8: 'Jubilee' class locomotive, No. 45682, passing Hasland Shed on the 'up' main line with an express passenger train. The shed roof was still intact at this time, but in later years the entire roof structure was removed as it became unsafe.

P. Hughes

Plate 9: A Class B freight train hauled by 8F, No. 48218, on the 'down' main line on Melton water troughs. It appears to be shut down so would not be picking up water on this occasion.

P. H. Groom

Plate 10: Passing Dore & Totley, No. 40537, a Class 2P 4-4-0 engine, gives yeoman service assisting an express up the bank from Sheffield, with a full head of steam.

B. Goodlad

Plate 11: Remembering my first trip on the 'Scotsman' in the Sheffield Blitz, this is how it would have looked. A Stanier 'Jubilee', No. 45622 *Nyasaland,* is pictured heading an express on the 'down' main line past Hasland Shed. Beyer-Garratts can be seen in the shed sidings. The water tank to the left of the picture was on top of our mess and locker rooms.

P. Hughes

Plate 12: The derailment, referred to in my story, which took place at Avenue Carbonisation Plant sidings more than 25 years ago. Our guard, Andy Anderson (on the left) is viewing the damage with some concern. I was driving the engine at the time.

A. Anderson

Plate 13: Fowler 'Royal Scot' 4-6-0, No. 46100, with the 'down Waverley' express passes Whittington on the old route heading north.

B. Handford

Plate 14: No. 41966, a Tilbury 4-4-2T, at Toton on 6 November 1955. At Hasland we nick-named these engines 'crooners'.

B. Goodlad

Plate 15: No. 44747, a Stanier Class 5, heading a Newcastle to Bristol express, charges out of the shor tunnel to the north of Sheffield in July 1955. This engine was fitted with Caprotti valve gear.

B. Goodla

Plate 16: Class 5, No. 44865, leaving Cowburn tunnel with a slow passenger train for Sheffield September 1955. After the next scheduled stop at Edale it would be travelling like an express train dov the high mountainous terrain to Hope Station.

B. Goodla

Plate 17: A view of the Sheffield Blitz showing trams burning near Change Alley and the Marples buildings in flames on 13 December 1940.

Brightside & Carbrook Co-op Society & Sheffield Library

Plate 18: The rescue of trapped persons from the bombed Marples Hotel in Sheffield after the air raids in December 1940.

Sheffield Newspapers & Sheffield Library

Plate 19: The Sheffield Blitz. The devastation in the High Street after the air raids of 12 December 1940.
Sheffield Newspapers & Sheffield Library

Plate 20: A 3F locomotive, No. 43211, hauling a Class A freight train of empty wagons from Gowholes sidings, slowly passes Dore & Totley West Junction.

P. Hughes

Plate 21: A Class 4F, No. 44089, with a full head of steam passes along the old route from Rotherham and heads south at Beighton. The steel bridge, overhead, was for the LNER. 26 June 1954.

B. Goodlad

Plate 22: Viaduct inspection. The North Eastern Region Civil Engineering Department checking the stonework, etc. on the Dunston and Barlow bridge over the River Whiting.

B. Chapman

Plate 23: An ex-LNWR 0-8-0, No. 49395, pictured in September 1956. After working a train of empty wagons from Gowholes to Tapton Junction the wagons would sometimes be propelled back down the 'old route' main line to Barrow Hill Sidings. The 'Wessie' No. 7 freight engine was not too popular with Midland men. One of these locomotives went through the shed wall at Hasland.

B. Chapman

Plate 24: Ivatt Class 2, No. 46502, at Barrow Hill Station on 5 July 1954. This was the last stopping passenger train to run over the old route from Sheffield to Chesterfield. To the rear is a double headed empty coach train approaching the station on the other line.

B. Goodlad

Plate 25: A Class 4 Ivatt locomotive, No. 43082, of Barrow Hill Shed (41E), arrives at Seymour Sidings, near Staveley, on 2 April 1965, with the Partington to Seymour empties.

B. Chapman

Plate 26: No. 46502, Ivatt 2-6-0, Class 2 locomotive pictured at Chesterfield on 5 July 1954 on the last slow passenger train to pass over the 'old route' from Sheffield to Chesterfield, via Holmes Junction, Kilmarsh and Barrow Hill. The engine is seen here standing in the 'up' passenger bay (south end). In the cab is driver Jim Woodhouse (left) and myself, the fireman (right).

B. Goodlad

Plate 27: Two Class 4F 0-6-0s, Nos. 44470 and 44425 standing at Barrow Hill Station with a train of empty coaches which had made up a Chesterfield, Barrow Hill, Skegness seaside special on 5 July 195

B. Goodla

Plate 28: An LMS 'Jubilee', No. 45608, with a full head of steam, heading north on the Dronfield ban The express would soon be shutting down in Bradway tunnel and enjoying the fast run down the othe side to Sheffield Station.

B. Chapma

Plate 29: An 8F freight, No. 48326, approaches Dore & Totley Station on the 'up' main line from Sheffield and hauls a heavy goods train through the snow on 27 February 1955.

B. Goodlad

Plate 30: Beyer-Garratt, No. 47971, bunker first, waits at the home signal outside the short Totley tunnel with a Class A empty wagon train for Avenue Sidings. Driver Dick Harrison is seen walking towards the signal box to 'sign the book' as required by Rule 55.

P. Hughes

Plate 31: Crab 2-6-0, No. 42849, with a heavy goods train near Great Longstone on 13 March 1953. In the background is seen the heavy smoke coming from the assisting 8F engine, No. 48500.

B. Goodla

Plate 32: Hasland Shed after the roof was completely removed. In the foreground is a BR Standard 2-10-0, No. 92135.

J. Phipp

a bit too heavy, and decided to rake it around. This would then ensure that when they finally arrived at the engine sheds the fire would be low and suitable for the engine disposal crew to clean. This young chap was 6ft. tall, young and fit. Without mentioning anything to his driver he climbed on to the tender to get the long rake. There was one more bridge to pass under before their train reached Avenue Sidings and this was the one that killed him. As he reached for the rake, the back of his head came in contact with the bridge and he was knocked face forward into the remaining bits of coal that were still on the tender. At the time the driver was unaware of this and was applying the engine brakes and looking out of the engine cab towards the sidings' signals. When he eventually looked back inside the cab and the on to the tender he was shocked to see his fireman lying in a crumpled position among the coal. Albert, tragically, was already dead, and a young lad's career had ended almost before it had begun.

We Midland men were not very keen on the 'Wessie' No. 7 freight engine. I personally could never feel comfortable with these 0-8-0 type locomotives, and must confess that I was a little frightened of them. There seemed hardly any room in the engine cab, and it was a work of art trying to shovel coal over those stupid, clumsy, round-shaped, brake or water scoop handles. I always finished up with damaged knuckles and bleeding fingers. The strange flap doors to the firebox didn't help me, and I would continually be littering the footplate with coal as I struggled to fire the locomotive.

I hated the injector arrangement and felt like a jack-in-a-box as I first opened the tender water valve in its low down position, and then reached up to the top of the engine cab for the injector steam valve. When the injector occasionally 'blew off', it was often with difficulty that I got them to work again.

I hope the 'Wessie' men will forgive me for criticising these engines, as they no doubt thought highly of them. It's a matter of use, I suppose. Here is an account of one of our drivers who shared my dislike of the 'Wessie'.

The engine was standing in Hasland Shed and the boiler was full to the whistle. This Midland driver refused to move her, and the foreman insisted that the engine should be taken out of the shed. We had a chap who had come to Hasland for promotion from a 'Wessie' shed. He scorned at my mate's dilemma and shouted out, 'what's wrong, are you bloody frightened of her?' I don't know whether my mate was afraid or just scared to death. Anyway, this gallant 'Wessie' driver climbed aboard and commenced to show us how it should be done.

The round turntable was turned in the direction of the 'Wessie', so everything was ready for the engine to be driven on to the turntable, turned round, and then driven out into the shed yard. Taking off the handbrake the 'Wessie' chap put the engine in fore gear, made sure that the cylinder cocks were wide open, and opened the regulator. The 'Wessie' took one gulp of some of the highly-filled boiler water and wham — away she galloped, right across the turntable, over the empty inspection pit opposite, finishing up through the shed wall! The poor old driver tried frantically to stop the locomotive, but all his efforts were in vain. It was brought home clearly to me that day that you cannot compress water.

On my holidays, a short time ago, I saw a painting of Holbeck engine shed in its heyday. A dangerous place an engine shed might be, but this painting captured everything; to me, it was a masterpiece. It depicted varying types of engines, sharp rays of sunlight streaming through the huge roof-ventilators, these rays trying to pierce the smoke which seemed to be always hanging around those old grimy buildings.

Fire irons were laying around the shed floor, barrow loads of clinker nearby; the artist seemed to have captured it all.

Enquiring about the cost of the painting I was told £900. This took me back a bit, and as a consolation I settled for a cheaper painting of a locomotive, which cost a few pounds.

There are many interesting books with good photographs of steam locomotives in them. I was looking at one of these recently and was thrilled to see No. 46502, an Ivatt class passenger tank engine. It was taken in Barrow Hill Station on the 'up' main line in 1954. This was the last stopping passenger train to run from Sheffield to Chesterfield via the 'old route'. I was the fireman on No. 46502 but my disappointment is that I didn't face the camera from my fireman's seat. I wish I had looked out when the photographs of the Ivatt engine and its coaches were taken. My mate was Jim Woodhouse, and as I recall, many photographs were taken on that historic occasion. However, I have been able to trace a photograph of myself and Jim Woodhouse with No. 46502 at Chesterfield (*Plate 26*).

A driver told me about an experience he had on an Avenue Sidings to Gowholes Sidings trip on which he had a Class 4 freight with a full train load of coal from Holmewood Colliery. At Unstone signal box the train was stopped, and they were instructed to shunt into the sidings. The signalman at Tapton Junction had reported seeing 'bodies' in one of the coal wagons, and the driver decided to investigate. Leaving the footplate he climbed into the first wagon of his train, levering himself up via the brake handle bracket and buffers, and peered over the top. Suddenly there was such a commotion — three or four uniformed figures jumped up, shouted something in what sounded to be German language and, leaping out of the wagons, ran off up the railway track. It appeared that they were German prisoners of war, who had escaped from a camp near Holmewood. They were trying to reach the Manchester or Liverpool dockland areas in their efforts to escape and return home. Old Reg told me that he was scared out of his wits, but was thankful that the Germans had not attacked him as he climbed on to the coal wagon. The signalman immediately reported that the prisoners were heading in the Dronfield direction. It was later learned that they were all recaptured in Dronfield village. This experience which old Reg had suffered was a far cry from another that I would like to mention.

You will, no doubt, have heard stories about steam drivers and firemen frying their breakfasts on the shovel. These are quite true, and the operation was usually very successful. A firing shovel had a blade which was long and slim and deep at the base; it was, indeed, like a frying pan with a very long handle. Painstakingly, crewmen would wash the shovel with the coal water slacking pipe, put it into the firebox doors, get it really hot, wash it down again, wipe it and, in the end, have a really shiny sterilised cooking utensil, they would then proceed to cook bacon, eggs, or whatever tasty morsel was available. Bearing in mind that rationing was in force, these things, however, always somehow seemed to be available. One could chat up a local farmer if the train was halted near his field — you know the picture — a piece of coal for a hen's egg. The smell of bacon frying would often cause other railwaymen to come over to our engine and pass some sort of comment. They probably had to manage with bread and cheese, and would have loved to have joined

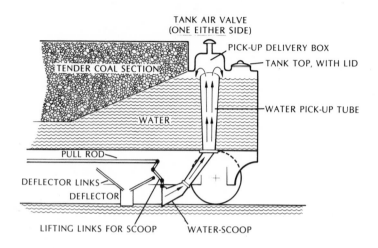

TANK AIR VALVE
(ONE EITHER SIDE)

PICK-UP DELIVERY BOX

TENDER COAL SECTION

TANK TOP, WITH LID

WATER PICK-UP TUBE

WATER

PULL ROD

DEFLECTOR LINKS

DEFLECTOR

LIFTING LINKS FOR SCOOP   WATER-SCOOP

A sketch of the water pick-up gear. When operated, the scoop lip touched the water (a little below the level). The deflector 'banked' up the water in front of the lip. Water was injected up the pick-up tube at high speed.

in the banquet that was taking place. A young fireman was once preparing his breakfast this way, when the driver 'accidentally' nudged the steam jet handle. The last this unfortunate young man saw of his breakfast was when it was quickly sucked into the firebox and really gobbled up — I bet he was more wary after that incident! No doubt, he would be hoping to get his own back on that driver who had deprived him of his breakfast. Who knows, he perhaps tried the same trick on some other 'greenhorn' later on. Many drivers were naturally full of the same sort of devilment, and the chap just mentioned was no exception.

Another bit of light-heartedness that sometimes happened was when a passenger train was leaving a station, like Leicester, for instance, it was more than likely that the tender water tank was full. It isn't far to the water troughs at Loughborough and, by then, very little water would have been consumed. One old driver used to look back at the coaches and see if there were any passengers with their heads sticking out of the front carriage windows. If there were, he would wait until we reached the troughs and tell me to drop the water scoop. With the water tank being almost full, the rush of water from the troughs would lift the tank lid and water would spurt all over the front coaches. It would be flying out of the tank air valves and all over the place. You can guess the rest — those poor unfortunate sightseers would think that rain storms really did come quickly in the Leicestershire area. It's a good job that tank lids had safety chains on, or I dread to think what would have happened otherwise.

The purpose of water troughs, of course, was to save trains stopping at water columns. This latter practice took a lot of time, especially with goods trains

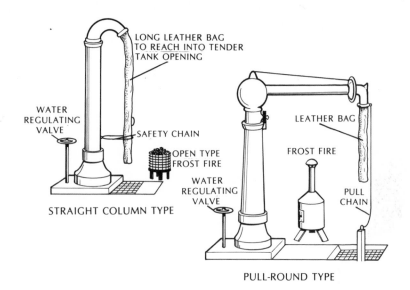

LONG LEATHER BAG
TO REACH INTO TENDER
TANK OPENING

WATER
REGULATING
VALVE

SAFETY CHAIN

OPEN TYPE
FROST FIRE

WATER
REGULATING
VALVE

STRAIGHT COLUMN TYPE

LEATHER BAG

FROST FIRE

PULL
CHAIN

PULL-ROUND TYPE

Two drawings of water columns.

that had to be carefully brought to a standstill, and after tanking up, slowly moved away before getting speed up again. Troughs were installed at Loughborough and Melton Mowbray, and several other strategic places. They were, naturally, on a good level stretch of line and this would give trains a chance to pick up speed to ensure a good force of water into the tender water scoop. The troughs were long and shallow, and drivers and firemen had to be on their mettle when using this method of tanking up. Under the engine tender was a water scoop which was hinged and which could be raised or lowered by the fireman, who would operate a large wheel fixed to the tender on the footplate. The driver would get up speed when approaching the troughs, the positions of which were indicated by a sign (illuminated at night). The water was forced up into the tank and the air in the tank, which was displaced, came out through two large air valves on the tender tank top. If a fireman was late in dropping the water scoop, the tank would probably end up only half full and, therefore, cause the driver added concern about how far that amount of water would take him. After picking up water, the scoop would then have to be quickly wound back, or it would be smashed or bent should it come into contact with any closing rails. There was always a safety chain fastened to the water scoop handle to ensure that this was not mistaken for the handbrake, and inadvertently lowered down and damaged. Often, when the drivers examined their engines, they would find water scoops that had been damaged. These would be reported immediately, but it wasn't always easy to find out just who did the damage. As mentioned earlier, most trains tanked up at the standing-type water columns. These were often positioned at the end of principal railway station platforms. Drivers, through their knowledge of the railways, knew where every water column was situated. During the winter months these were often frozen up, and to try to eliminate this, frost fires were placed at all water column standards. These were kept alight by station staff, platelayers and footplatemen whenever possible. In the more lonely areas, sometimes no other staff was available. Locomotive crews were then expected to 'keep the home fires burning' with coal from their engine tenders. Thus, they would make sure that sufficient coal was left for restoking should the platelayers be passing by.

Stopping at a water column, on one occasion, we noticed that the fire had been neglected. Consequently, the column and water bag were frozen stiff. We just could not pull it round. We were so short of water that my driver was prepared to try anything. He fastened the chain around the tender handrail and eased the engine forward. This did the trick and the crane moved round. Whilst we were tanking up, I shovelled some hot fire out of our engine firebox and put this into the frost-fire brazier. Then we put a lot of coal on top to ensure the fire would last until the next train arrived.

Stories have been told about water columns actually getting pulled down or broken when they have become frozen and drivers have tried to liberate them.

Here is a short tale about the danger of throwing coal from engine tenders.

On a local passenger run with a No. 2 passenger engine, we were going steadily up the bank through Broomhouse Tunnel and approaching Unstone on the Sheffield route. Suddenly, from behind a small bush, a small girl appeared, it was obvious that she was begging for coal, and we were surprised that her parents had encouraged her to do this. It was just after 7a.m. so it seemed unlikely that the child had planned it herself. However, our hearts went out to the child and we duly supplied her with several lumps of coal. These broke into pieces as soon as they hit the side of the track. The next day, on the same trip, we again spotted the child, so we prepared to help her again. Imagine our horror, when, just as we were about to drop some large lumps of coal, we noticed that the child had brought some other children with her. Fortunately the coal was still on the footplate, or heaven knows what the consequences might have been. This was another lesson learned — do not encourage anyone to trespass on to railway lines.

Later, on that same run, we noticed a small boy running down the steep bank side, and a big dog was chasing behind him. Realising that the bank was getting steeper, the lad veered off to a safer part of the ground. Unfortunately, the dog was running much too fast and tried, with fateful consequences, to run in front of our engine. One day we were hauling wagons from Avenue Sidings to Bonds Main Colliery; it was on an uphill gradient and my mate was determined that the colliery would get its empty trucks on time. We had a Class 4 freight and about 30 empty wagons on our train. Charging out of a short single line tunnel, under the main Grassmoor road, we saw a wooden sleeper had been placed across the railway lines. My driver instinctively shut down steam, then quickly opened up the regulator again. The front wheels of our engine hit the obstruction and there was firewood for everyone. The sleeper was smashed to smithereens. This was a bit of quick thinking, and it's doubtful if the guard at the rear knew anything about it. Had the driver panicked, he could have seriously injured the guard, who could have been knocked almost out of his brake van. We were thankful that it had not caused a derailment which, in those circumstances, could have been horrific. The engine was at the outer end of the tunnel and the rear wagons and guard's brake would, at the time of the impact, have been well out of the other side.

A similar incident of quick thinking, but this time on a passenger train, was when a Leeds driver was driving an express train and travelling at full speed.

Rounding a bend on the line he saw, to his amazement, that the track ahead was distorted. He immediately shut down steam but didn't apply the vacuum brake at once. Only when the engine went in to the bent track did he steadily apply the brake. The driver said that the leading coach became derailed. Afterwards, at the enquiry, the driver was commended for his quick thinking. His engine had, in fact, 'straightened' out the track. He was told that if he had applied the brake instantly the whole train could have been derailed. The driver ended his story by saying that, for a long time afterwards, his fireman had a particular sort of fear whenever they approached that section of the line.

In the winter of 1947, railwaymen worked long shifts in appalling conditions. Trains became snowed under for more than a day, at times. In many cases, engine fires had to be thrown out when the tender tanks had run out of water. It snowed endlessly for days. When using the snowploughs — being pushed by two or three engines, these would often come to a standstill — such was the depth of snow. Troops were often asked to assist platelayers to dig out in those freak conditions. At home, people didn't know where to clear the snow to, and eventually they gave up trying, and looked forward to the day when it would cease.

Driving or firing engines on the Derbyshire Peak line in those conditions could be a nightmare. On that same section it was a fantastic and awesome sight to see the huge icicles that hung from the entrance to Dore, Totley and Cowburn tunnels. The entrances were like castles with their portcullises down. Engine crews were sensible enough not to put their heads outside the engine cabs. The blast from engine chimneys would smash the huge icicles to the ground, the pointed lumps of ice actually embedding themselves into the floorboards on the footplate. When the platelayers were called to remove these dangerous obstructions, they could fill wagon loads with icicles. Mountain sheep were found frozen inside the tunnels after venturing inside for protection from the heavy snows. In the later months, there was heavy flooding, and here is a story about an unusual flooding incident.

We had No. 4294, a Hasland No. 4 freight engine, and again we were working a train from Avenue Sidings to Gowholes Sidings. Approaching Hope Station, on the Peak line, the skies were beginning to get very black. There was thunder rumbling around the hills and the clouds seemed to be hanging unusually low. Passing Earles Cement Works Sidings and climbing up to Edale, the No. 4 freight was going beautifully. This was to be one of the better days. Then the rains came and it really belted it down. The coal on the tender was of the small type, consisting of a lot of slack. Rain poured off the shovelling plate, and at times I seemed to be firing with slush. In fact, it was possible to continually tilt the shovel and allow water to fall off it. No. 4294 loved the slush and continued to steam freely. My mate was delighted and caused me to have a little chuckle; he had taken off his cap. He was bald-headed and rain was running off his 'pippin'. 'Whatever is going on', I laughingly asked — 'didn't you know' was the reply —'rain makes your hair grow'. Fortunately I have always been blessed with a good head of hair, so I kept my own hat firmly pulled on, and paid full attention to firing the engine.

The signalman at Cowburn slowed us down at the signals and, as we passed his signalbox, he shouted 'proceed at caution — there is temporary flooding of the line at the other end of Cowburn Tunnel'. He lowered the starter signal so off we went. Anybody who knows this area will tell you that from Cowburn Tunnel to Chinley there is a very steep gradient. However was it possible to have temporary flooding of the line on a gradient? Cautiously we finally reached the Chinley end of Cowburn Tunnel. We could hardly believe our eyes. Rushing past the entrance at great depth were torrents of fast moving water. My mate, Albert, cautiously let the train roll and, coming out of the tunnel, we got a real battering from the force of rushing water. Looking back we saw water almost bouncing over our trailing wagons. It was an amazing experience. The signalman asked if it was safe to let a train pass on the opposite line. He had a slow passenger train standing at his home signal and wanted some advice. My mate wouldn't commit himself as he didn't know if the ballast was getting washed away from the opposite railway sleepers. On our return journey we received a detailed explanation of this unusual happening from the old ganger in charge of permanent way repairs. It appears that there is a man-made gulley down the side of the tunnel which continues under the railway lines, turning right and then down the back of the signal box. The sheer force of water was too much for the underground gulley to take, so it rushed up and over the line. The water that followed increased in height and volume. It obviously couldn't last long and as soon as the storm abated, it would ease off as quickly as it had begun. The old ganger said that in all his forty years on the railroad this was the most spectacular experience that he had witnessed. Platelayers had to renew missing ballast and, for a time, trains passed to and fro at caution.

There is an amazing ending to this story. On our return journey when I called at the signal box to sign for Rule 55, the signalman was feeding milk to a little kitten. He told me that the poor little mite came down with the water. 'There isn't a farm around for miles', he added. That surely is a case of a cat with nine lives!

The 1947 floods bring back other memories. After the snow, the heavy flooding was the worst for years in the Nottingham area; the River Trent reached an all time high depth of water. We should have worked our usual slow passenger train from Chesterfield to Nottingham but the Control decided to cancel a lot of these and allow only a skeleton service. Jack Taft and myself were on one of these few trains.

Approaching Long Eaton Junction there was a fair depth of water around the crossing gates. This was the same at Attenborough and Beeston, but things didn't seem too bad, and we wondered what all the fuss was about. After leaving Beeston Station we were stopped at Lenton Junction, and a Railway Inspector, dressed in black overcoat and a black bowler, climbed aboard our footplate. He instructed us to make sure that we had a good head of steam, plenty of fire in the box, and we were to firmly close the damper. We were under his personal supervision — we should ignore all signals and proceed cautiously as far as Nottingham Station, where we were to carry on to the furthest end of the platform before allowing our passengers to disembark. Leaving Lenton, we could hardly believe our own eyes, as the entire area in front of us was covered with water. Men in boats were pushing debris out of our way and there was flotsam everywhere. Planks of new wood were floating away from a nearby timber yard, and barrels from a local factory had been floated up and over the factory boundary fence. After the floods had subsided, people found some very strange things in their back gardens!

To give you some idea of the depth of water, the rail point handles were not visible. We more or less worked on the single line principle because our engine was throwing water about like a speedboat. Fortunately, the damper was a good fit and the fire was not affected.

Chapter Four

TRAGIC ACCIDENTS AND HAIR-RAISING INCIDENTS

Some really bad accidents happened and the worst fatality that I personally witnessed was in Leicester Station. After working the Leeds to Leicester goods train with a Class 9 freight, we disposed of our engine at the shed, and were then instructed to go to the station platform and ring Control for instructions. It was slightly foggy, visibility wasn't very good and we were carefully making our way towards the sloping end of Leicester (Midland) Station. A railcar unit was approaching from the Loughborough direction and had reached a point about a quarter of the way up the platform when the brake went on fully. We were about to pass remarks that the driver would knock his passengers off their feets when looking down we saw the pitiful figure of a young woman lying across one of the rails, having been struck by the train. It was the worst experience of my life and I was stunned and shocked. For weeks afterwards I could see her face, and my driver said that the experience had the same effect on him.

Forgive me for mentioning this incident, but who are the brave people who cope with such situations? Within minutes screens were placed all around. It's doubtful if the passengers on the platform knew anything untoward had happened. We were later told that the girl had committed suicide and that the only warning the driver had was when he saw 'something' pass in front of his cab window. A businessman reported that he had seen the girl take a calculated jump.

There were many funny and unfortunate happenings on the railway from time to time, here is just one. A train was standing at the 'up' goods line signal at Canklow Locomotive Shed signal box, the signal was at danger, and it was intended that the signalman was going to first let trains proceed on the 'up' main line before allowing this goods train to follow them. The goods line signal was on the left of our unfortunate driver's engine, and the main line signal was on the right. He must have been dozing and, looking up, saw a signal for go. Opening the engine regulator he moved his train on. Unfortunately he had seen the main line signal and thought that it was the one he wanted. Not until he had almost landed on top of a rubbish tip did he learn his mistake. It caused quite a commotion as other trains were behind him and they had also moved along.

Here is a similar occurrence, but with fatal consequences. Older drivers used to tell us about a Bescot train which was travelling from Clay Cross on the 'up' main line to Morton. There was a more important train in the section behind, so the signalman at Morton decided to shunt the Bescot train out of

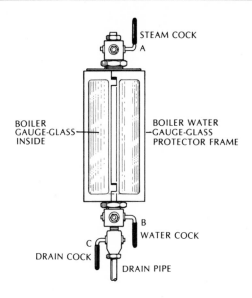

STEAM COCK
A

BOILER
GAUGE-GLASS
INSIDE

BOILER WATER
GAUGE-GLASS
PROTECTOR FRAME

B
WATER COCK

C
DRAIN COCK

DRAIN PIPE

A sketch of the boiler water gauge principal. If the glass broke, A and B cocks would be closed at once.

the way of the following train. After the special train had passed by, it was decided to let the Bescot train follow on. Then the signalman made a terrible mistake — after pulling up several sets of points, he allowed the train to proceed towards Doe Hill and Tibshelf. Not until it got to Doe Hill Station did the Bescot driver realise what was wrong — his train was going down the 'down' main line instead of the 'up' main. Far away in the distance a double-headed express train was coming from the Westhouses direction, also on the 'down' main line. It must have been a nightmare situation — what could they do? In those circumstances they would obviously try to stop their train, but would have to bail out and get as far away as possible. I don't know the full story, but the oncoming express charged into this Bescot train and lives were lost, including those of the footplatemen on the express.

This was a dreadful occurrence and something that drivers would probably only ever dream about. Accidents like these made railway personnel doubly sure that they would try to avoid them ever happening again. We were taught all the protection rules and regulations but, unfortunately, in the case just mentioned, there wasn't time for anybody to do anything to avoid the fatal collision.

Often, when travelling along, gauge glasses would burst. They had a protective case of extra strong glass around them but, nevertheless, bits would fly and it could be pretty frightening. Sometimes glasses would give prior warning and start to leak — at other times they would just go off with a bang. If you have ever been in a car when the windscreen shatters, you will have had a similar experience, except that in the case of our gauge glass, steam and boiling water gushed out all over the place. We would quickly try to close both top and bottom gauge frame valves and shut down the water and steam. It wasn't difficult to fit a new glass and, as previously stated, these were kept in a safe place on the footplate.

On a shunt engine, on one occasion, we had a similar experience, except that the engine was a closed cab type. It was dark and we were taken by surprise. The engine cab quickly filled up with steam and both of us had to put our heads outside. After several attempts we finally managed to find the shut-off cocks and stop the pressure, which was only achieved by first throwing an overcoat over the damaged gauge glass and frame. Engine injectors sometimes caused problems and the clacks would stick open, allowing steam to fly out at full pressure from the overflow pipe, which was usually fixed near the bottom step. Grabbing the coal pick and using the square flat end, it was the practice to sharply tap the top of the clack box; this sharp jolt would cause the sticking clack to reseat, and all was well again. If this method failed, the steam plug would have to be closed, but then the injector was obviously shut off. The purpose of the steam clack was to allow water to be passed from the tender tank into the boiler, via the injector. The injectors were used to deliver water into the boiler. They had three cones; a steam cone, a combining cone and a delivery cone. When the fireman opened the water valve from the tender tank he also opened the steam valve on the engine. A jet of steam emerging at high velocity from the steam cone would be brought into contact with the cold water. Partial condensation in the steam jet took place, a partial vacuum was formed, and the water was drawn forward at speed into the combining cone at the wide end. It left the small end at high speed, and from here it would go into the delivery cone and then via the clack into the boiler. Once, on a return journey from York, the clack stuck on the injector of our No. 8 freight taper boiler type locomotive. This happened at Pontefract, and steam was blowing full bore. The clack on these locomotives was on top of the boiler and, therefore, it was impossible for us to try to knock it down on to its face. We operated the other injector but were finding it difficult to maintain full steam pressure. All signals were in the clear position, and our train consisted of empty ironstone wagons, so we plodded on.

Arriving at Canklow, and stopping under the protection of signals, the driver asked for a fitter from the nearby Canklow Shed. This fellow sat astride the boiler top and, with the pointed end of the coal pick, attempted to try to reseat the clack. All his efforts were in vain, so we unhooked the engine and it was taken into Canklow engine shed. Another No. 8 freight engine was available and this enabled us to get back to our train on the goods line and couple up and carry on our journey to Clay Cross.

I once saw a clack become stuck on a big passenger engine. The driver uncoupled from the coaches, rushed his engine forward, tried stopping quickly, and did the same coming back, but to no avail. He also tried bouncing the engine wheels off a fishplate. Again this was an isolated incident and the only time I personally had encountered it was with the No. 8 freight.

Danesmoor Colliery in Derbyshire has been closed for years now, and the old terraced houses in the nearby village are no longer standing; in fact it is simply just a 'ghost town'. This is a far cry from the days when the mine was working at full capacity. To take wagons to this colliery could be quite an experience. The empty coal trucks had to be propelled up a steep incline, so that the colliery shuntman could lower them down, when required, under the screens; they would then be topped up with coal and lowered away to eventually complete trains, which would be taken to various parts of the country. Setting back into the dead end at the Morton end we would raise full steam, and attempt to propel some thirty empty wagons up the incline. The shunter would ride in the last wagon and, as soon as he was told that the crossing was clear of traffic, would wave his arms for us to proceed. We would set off, sanders fully open and the whistle blowing to warn that we were on our way. Sparks would really be flying from the engine chimney, and this courageous man in the last wagon would be frantically calling us on. Reaching the section of railway lines in the colliery area, would often cause the engine to slip, as grime and dirt had drifted on to these rail surfaces. Often when the sanders were not working properly we had to set right back and start all over again. When we were successful, and got the wagons to the summit, it was laughable to see the shunter quickly jump out of that last truck — he didn't intend going over the top of the bank.

A Hasland driver was working a train from Nottingham to Derby, and it was a slow passenger train and his engine was probably a No. 2 passenger type. Approaching Spondon, he had his head out of the engine cab and was applying the vacuum brake; then wham! — he was hit in the face by an object. Some lads were larking about on the footbridge and had 'bombarded' him, and unfortunately their direct hit had landed in the driver's eye. Stopping the train he went to the signal box, phoned Control and asked for a relief driver to be ready to take over at Derby Station. Going back to his footplate and, by now, in great pain, he somehow managed to continue on to Derby and get some medical attention.

The poor man nearly lost the sight of one of his eyes and he was off work for months; he finally had to take a job in the stores. When the railway police went to Spondon they caught the culprits and confiscated their 'ammunition'; they had been throwing apples at passing trains.

If younger train spotters read this they might realise what a dangerous practice throwing objects at trains can be. It might even lead to more serious consequences than the one just mentioned.

Chapter Five

TRIP WORKINGS AND DUTIES

Younger readers may think, after reading some of these reminiscences, we didn't travel very far on our goods trains in a day's work. To help them understand, here is a typical short trip that we often worked — Chesterfield to Rowsley; a distance of about 24 miles.

Let us assume that we had to start from Staveley Sidings; not far down the line. First, we would have to prepare our engine at Hasland; this would take about an hour. Then, with our guard, we would proceed light engine to Staveley for our train. On reaching the sidings, the guard would examine his train, making sure that all the wagons were properly labelled and coupled up. If any wagon brake rods had dropped down, he would lift these up and secure them in the brackets with the cotter-pins. Finally, he would tell the driver of what the train comprised, and if any wagons were to be detached or picked up en route, and the sidings staff would inform the signalman when all was ready to go. From a dead start with a heavy train there could be difficulty in getting the train out of the sidings. A lot of engine slipping may be encountered, so it was always an advantage if the train could be stationed on an open 'road'. This gave the shunt engine a chance to get to the rear and give trains a 'kick' up the backside out on to the main line. Main line traffic was pretty regular on this section and during the war many troop trains, etc. would be given priority. Eventually our train would be out on the main line, heading up to the Tapton Junction. Here again delays could be encountered, as trains approached from both the Staveley and Dronfield directions.

Perhaps I ought to mention places of interest as we go along, as again this might be of interest to the younger reader.

Tapton House was the home of George Stephenson, the British Engineer and railway pioneer. He became a plant engineer, invented a safety lamp and designed and built colliery locomotives. In 1821, he was appointed Engineer to the Stockton & Darlington Railway; he became Chief Engineer to the Liverpool & Manchester Railway (1826), and laid the line during the next three years. In 1826, his own locomotive *The Rocket* won the Rainhill 'Trial', and the Directors' £500 prize. In 1823, he established his own locomotive works at Newcastle. His son, Robert Stephenson, designed bridges and railways, the Britannia Tubular Bridge (Menai Strait), the Conway Bridge, and the Victoria Bridge (Montreal) being among his notable works.

Tapton House is high on the hill at Tapton, and cannot be clearly seen from the railway. Leaving Tapton with our train, we would soon pass the town of Chesterfield with its famous crooked spire. This is part of the Parish Church of St. Mary and All Saints. The present Church replaced an earlier Saxon one — the building began at the East End and this portion was dedicated as early as 1234. It was extended westwards in 1375 and 1400, it is 228ft. high and leans 8ft. 7in. to the south, 9ft. 4in. to the south-west, and 3ft. 9in. to the west. It is crooked as a result of the use of unseasoned timber and the extremes of temperature, coupled with the weight of 50 tons of lead on its exterior.

We would be hoping that we were on the main line, and heading quickly up to Clay Cross, passing Hasland engine shed on our left.

Heading up to Clay Cross Tunnel with its fortress-like opening, we might again encounter slipping, but would hope that the sanding apparatus was working properly. Arriving at Stretton, we would again encounter delay and be shunted on to the loop line to allow more important trains to pass. During our stay on these loop lines, all sorts of engines would pass during the war years; engines from other companies that had brought troop trains, etc. from the far corners of Britain. It could be a train spotters' paradise, but train spotters were not as much in evidence as they are today. To our right would be the old Ashover Light Railway, and further right, the impressive Stretton Hall. Running down to South Wingfield, and approaching the tunnel, we would see the ruins of Wingfield Manor. It was here that Mary, Queen of Scots, passed a great deal of her time in captivity under the custody of the Earl of Shrewsbury. The Manor was greatly damaged in the Civil Wars, and in 1646 was dismantled by order of Parliament.

At Crich Junction, trains again converged; Westhouses, Toton or Kirkby men would be working trains from the Butterley direction (this is where the Butterley Preservation Society is today, at Swanwick). Hopefully, we would be allowed to proceed ahead of these trains, or time would really be passing by.

If we did get priority we would continue on to the Ambergate triangular station. This was an impressive structure, solely constructed of wood, and the station buildings were high up over several roads. To our left was the 'old' Ambergate Station and Toad Mar Tunnel. The old station was built around 1840 and was replaced by the wooden one around 1876. Here again a delay could occur as trains approached from the Derby direction. Going on our way we would see the 'Crich Stand' on our right. This is a memorial to the Sherwood Foresters; it resembles a lighthouse and is lit up at night, and which can clearly be seen for miles around. At Crich today there is the famous tramway museum, and this attracts thousands of visitors from all over the country.

Passing on to Whatstandwell, there was an unusual feature. The canal was above us, the main road below and, at the bottom, was the River Derwent. These four features ran parallel for quite a distance.

After Whatstandwell and its pretty little garden station we would pass Lea Hurst, the one-time home of Florence Nightingale. The next place was High Peak Junction, this was a single line track up to Middleton Top and served the local quarries. This connected with Buxton, Wirksworth and Uttoxeter. We never went on to that section, other than just to put wagons off and pick up on our return at High Peak.

Picking up speed and passing over a large steel-structured bridge over the Derwent River, the train now approached Cromford Sidings signal box. This was about the last place that we could again be shunted before reaching Darley Dale. We were always pleased if the distant signal was lowered because we could then have a run at Willersley Tunnel, just out of Cromford Station. This was an uphill section and when travelling slowly we could encounter 'slipping'. The station buildings at Cromford were very impressive, and the rockery-type bank sides were well looked after. Soon the train would pass through Matlock Bath Station, and there were then a few very short tunnels, these passing under High Tor which was about 300ft. above. Matlock Bridge Station was then reached after passing over the road bridge. Nowadays, every year towards autumn they have the Venetian Lights at Matlock and Matlock Bath, and visitors come to see these from all over the country. There isn't a better place to put on a show like this, the river, which winds through the centre, gives added reflection to the coloured lights. There are inumerable cafes, restaurants and gift shops along the promenade, and it is well worth a visit.

After Matlock there was Darley Dale and then Rowsley sidings. Even at Church Lane Crossing, at Darley Dale, we could again be shunted out of the way. This nearly always happened, and we would not depart until Rowsley Sidings could deal with our train.

Here is a short story about Darley Dale; we were told that the Romans had a camp on the hillside. The story I like to remember was about a solitary tree on the horizon to our left. There was supposed to be a wealthy landowner who had lost his son. The lad had died, and the man planted this tree in memory of his son.

The station buildings on that line certainly had character, and it would be nice to think that if the Matlock and Rowsley preservation societies get their way and obtain that stretch of line, they will see that these buildings are also preserved. At Rowsley Sidings, the engine would finally be unhooked and would be driven back to the engine sheds to be turned round. Rowsley Shed was of the straight type, and the buildings ran parallel. Outside, it had the turntable. In those days, passengers would alight at Rowsley for Chatsworth House, the home of the Duke and Duchess of Devonshire; it was also a stopping place for anyone wanting to visit Haddon Hall. There always appeared to be a lot of 'Wessie' engines at Rowsley; these must have drifted in from the Uttoxeter line, just mentioned, and from the 'Wessie' section. Another engine that was in prominence was the 'Crab' type Midland 2-6-0 mixed traffic locomotive. To end our Rowsley trip we would finally pick up wagons for Avenue Sidings and return home. Very often this short trip of perhaps 40 miles from start to finish would take six or seven hours. After disposing of the locomotive at the shed we would make our way home.

This is a far cry from today's operations. Avenue Sidings and Rowsley are overgrown with weeds, and the engine sheds at Hasland and Rowsley are just a railway memory.

One night we had signed on duty at midnight. This was one of the severest winters that I had known. It snowed endlessly for days and days, and after that there were severe freezing conditions. Our duties on this particular evening were to prepare engines for train crews who would be signing on duty right through the night and early morning. It was freezing hard, and it was our task to get the engines out into the yard in order of departure. They had to be fully coaled up, oiled and watered. Most of the shed roof at Hasland had already been removed for safety reasons, and the place looked like some ruins from the bygone days. Snow had previously fallen all around the shed, and we were paddling about in the stuff as we went about our duties. This particular night it was hard and icy, and had frozen solid to the sides of the shed floor. Water all over the rest of the floor had turned to ice and the place was like a skating rink.

We worked like navvies, trying to get the engines on to the turntable and eventually out of the shed to the locomotive yard. The engine wheels were frozen solid on to the rails. The same had happened to the steel wheels on the turntable, and we used large tommy bars to prise under the wheels. Even when my driver had given the engines steam, some of them refused to move. We tried reversing the frozen locomotives and it was push and shove all the way. The fitters were 'toffs' that night, and helped us all they could. They had enough on their slates as it was, and one could not help but admire their cheerfulness when working in such appalling conditions.

Moving engines was going to be the least of our worries, as the main worry was that injectors had become frozen. Icicles were hanging from the overflow pipes, tender valves were frozen and, all in all, it was a desperate situation that we were in. We tried to defrost these frozen pipes by putting lighted soaked paraffin rags all around them. Out in the locomotive yard we made coal fires at intervals; some were in large braziers, and others just heaps of fire on the ground. Wherever possible, we finally stationed engines with their injectors and overflow pipes near to these fires. We were up and down on footplates like 'yo-yos'. In an isolated case we actually decided to throw out an engine fire. The water could not be seen in the boiler gauge glass, even with the bottom gland loosened and lifted up. Time was all important, so we took no chances and shovelled the fire out of that particular engine on to the ground. At least the fire was doing another engine some good, and helping to defrost it.

Moments like these bring the best out of people, they say. One thing is certain, we knew who our friends were that night. Other than the fitters, I would like to pay tribute to the foreman fitter, old Bill. He was a big, powerful fellow, and was capable of standing in the inspection pits and bodily lifting engine springs into position. Fitters would stand by to insert the fastening pins into the spring hangers, whilst Bill held them aloft. If the operation was not done quickly he would drop the spring back on to the floor and the dilatory fitter would hear the length of the foreman fitter's tongue. These engine shed gangs deserved all the praise they got for their efforts in such primitive and dangerous conditions.

One evening, a Hasland driver was working a train on a local branch line. Along with his fireman, he went into a nearby bus garage canteen for a quick cup of tea. On their return to the footplate, they were shocked and amazed to find that all their remaining coal had been taken from the small tank's bunker. Scrounging some coal from a platelayer's cabin further down the line, they then unhooked their engine and went back to Hasland Shed for sufficient coal to carry on with their branch work operations. No doubt, after this little episode, they would be reluctant to leave their post and, if it was at all necessary to do so, would leave a 'sentry' on guard.

There have been similar stories told about engines working on colliery premises. Engine crews have gone into the colliery canteens, overstayed their lunch sessions and returned to find the fire had died out in the firebox. In cases such as these, the knowledge gained from their earlier steam-raising tuition would really be needed.

Here is a joke that was passed around the relief cabins. Four drunks staggered on to a railway station platform; the train was about to leave. Three of the chaps managed to tumble aboard and the fourth was hanging on to the carriage door, the train dragging him along the platform. As the train was picking up speed, station staff pulled the unfortunate chap clear. Then, to their amazement, he started to laugh. 'It isn't funny', remarked a porter — 'you could have been killed'. 'Oh, I'm not laughing about that', the man replied and, pointing a finger said, 'it's my three buddies on the train — they only came to see me off'.

An old driver always seemed to be eating bread and marmalade for his lunch. He had never married so perhaps had to put up with this situation because he was in lodgings. Just for fun I said to him, 'I am surprised that you eat that stuff — they give it to the troops when they are stationed abroad, it stops them from getting over amorous and letting down their wives who are at home; it has the same effect as bromide'. 'Is that a fact', the driver laughingly exclaimed and, throwing the remaining sandwiches outside the cab doors, shouted 'bugger the marmalade'. I really should not have teased him because he then helped me to finish off my sandwiches. The following Saturday evening, on a run to York, he opened his 'snap bag' and produced the biggest newspaper parcel that you could imagine. Thrusting this into my hands he said, 'here you are, have a go at that'. Opening the newspaper and the greaseproof piece inside, I was amazed to see a pile of cold fish and chips. These were crudely slapped between two thick slices of bread. I enjoyed the bread and the piece of cold fish — but cold chips — never!

In a more serious vein, one of the drivers at Hasland was a bit of a philosopher. I will never forget old Harry when he repeated two famous quotations. The first — 'Hell hath no fury like a woman scorned' — how true that could sometimes be when, perhaps, a fireman had not turned up for a date and his impatient girlfriend had later given him a taste of her pent-up frustrations. In lots of cases the unfortunate chap was perhaps miles away on the footplate, working overtime. Then the second quotation — 'man's inhumanity to man makes countless thousands mourn' — how true that is in these times of unrest throughout the so-called civilized world.

We often lodged in the barracks at Wellingborough. These buildings were situated almost on top of the railway bridge. When we were inside the place we could hear almost every train that passed by. Added to that, the express train drivers kicked up a hell of a din with their whistles wide open as they thundered through Wellingborough Station close by.

After washing, eating, and finally turning in, we would try our best to get some sleep. Throughout the night and day one could hear first one and then another of the drivers, firemen and guards being roused from their beds. However, if the stewards could get us a cubicle at the far end of the building that might help us to sleep through some of these disturbances.

On certain available turns of duty, before going to bed, we often went into the town at Wellingborough. Old Charlie, one of my mates, was a giant of a man. He never seemed to have problems with his sleeping, especially after downing seven or eight pints of southern ale. In fact, on our return, I am sure that his snoring could be heard through the length and breadth of the barracks. Charlie used to fancy a certain landlady and, given the chance, would willingly have sacrificed his bed at the barracks for a place in her bed.

This loss of sleep often made me feel lethargic on the return journey, and on sections of the line when the regulator was shut down it was with difficulty that I was able to keep my eyes open.

There used to be a tale about a locomotive crew going on a journey to Burton. Their train was stopped at signals near to a canal bridge. The driver noticed a young couple kissing and cuddling on the bank side. Cheekily, he said to his fireman, 'go and see what that pair are up to'. The fireman did as he was told. When he returned he informed his mate that the couple were up to their tricks and having a right good time. The driver couldn't conceal his curiosity so he climbed down from the footplate and went to have a peep for himself. He very quickly returned, and was holding his handkerchief to his head. 'What's wrong', enquired his mate — the driver groaned, and still holding his head replied, 'that young chap down there; he caught me watching them, and jumped up and belted me'. 'I thought he might do', chuckled the fireman, 'he tried to hit me when he knew I was watching them'.

After working a goods train and being relieved by Derby men, we walked from St. Mary's Junction to Derby Station. There was an empty coach in the lay-by next to platform No. 1. Suddenly, without any apparent warning, the coach started moving, and had it carried on too far, I thought that it would foul the main line. It was a guard's-type van, with the handbrake inside. I dropped my haversack on the permanent way, jumped on to the step, opened the carriage door and diving inside quickly applied the brake. Jumping down and feeling quite proud of myself I said to my driver, 'what about that mate'? A man from the other side of the coach could be heard shouting 'what blithering idiot put the brake on', Apparently, there were several men at the opposite end pushing the thing. With great expedience, I made a tactful departure.

Here is another incident which may be of interest, and which I highlight to point out that there were many other 'movements' by the side of the track, other than those made by passing trains.

One evening, my fireman, guard and I were walking by the lineside up to the local colliery sidings. The guard was leading the way, swinging his lighted paraffin lamp as he went along. He stopped rather suddenly and pointing his light at a clump of grass exclaimed, 'what's that'! The light was shining on a tiny fieldmouse, and the little creature was petrified and transfixed by the bright light. It was almost standing up on its back legs, and was clutching what appeared to be a wild berry of some sort. Picking up his foot the guard prepared to drop his heavy boot on the unfortunate little creature, when my mate restrained him. 'The little bugger's done you no harm — leave it', my mate shouted. 'I can't stand the bloody things', the guard irritatingly replied. While the two were arguing, and the light was turned away for a moment or two, the mouse sensibly scurried away to the safety of the embankment.

Looking back on some of the stories, I would not like the reader to think that all of our railway trips were cosy ones. In the early days, as a youth, I suffered the embarrassment of many a driver's sarcasm. One could not expect a 'greenhorn' to give the same performance as an experienced fireman. After about four or five years of firing duties, a fireman would be capable of holding his own with most men. Some of the critical drivers would never be prepared to admit that they often contributed to bad trips. They would have been offended if the boot was on the other foot and the firemen told them that they couldn't 'drive' an engine, let alone fire one. Firemen have confided in me that, from the moment they climbed on to the footplate, certain drivers upset them. When driving engines myself I liked to think that I was not in this category, and always tried to give my mates confidence.

On many occasions firemen have been 'down the nick' for steam, lack of experience in the early stages and poor steamers not making things any better for them. As a lad, trying to combat the swaying movement of a locomotive at speed and the anxiety of failing to maintain steam, often made me feel inadequate. The heat from the searing firebox and the heavy firing duties often made me realise that this wasn't a job for the faint-hearted. If the tube plate was fired up with the 'bird's nests' of scale that I mentioned earlier, heat from the firebox could be unbearable, the blocked tubes allowing the intense heat back to the fire hole doors. In these instances it was a good idea to keep shirt and overall sleeves rolled down to protect one's arms from getting burned, and the hairs singed off them.

Hasland wasn't a glamorous shed and, like the poor cousins, we didn't possess the big sophisticated engines often seen in railway magazines. On our seaside excursions to Morecambe in the summer months we had to make do with Class 4 freight engines and, if we didn't prepare for these faster runs in good time, we would pay for it. With the Class 4 freights, as the train increased in speed, particles of ash that fell into the ashpan would be shuffled out on to the track. The speed of the train and the sudden rush of air under the engine would induce some of these particles to blow up into the engine cab. It was bad enough then, to be wiping the sweat off, but if we were faced with this sudden upsurge of dust, we would soon be resembling coal miners. Lots of our lads put neckerchiefs around their necks and buttoned their overall collars up. Some wore the old cloth caps pulled well down over their eyes, others elected to wear berets, and some possessed goggles. To minimise the hazard mentioned above, we used to get to the shed in good time and dig a number of grass sods out of the embankment. Taking these up on to the footplate, we would wedge them over the offending gaps under the fire hole door, and right round the bottom of the boiler face plate. Then, with the slacking pipe, we would saturate the grass and soil until it was like one big sponge. This would act as a 'draught excluder', but it was necessary to continually keep damping the sods down, otherwise they would soon dry out with the heat from the firebox, and the rush of air from under the engine. I know that our sods made the footplate untidy and the place looked like a stable but, nevertheless, it was well worth it.

Chapter Six

BEYER-GARRETT WORKINGS

Dronfield Bank was always a test of a fireman's ability; the very heavy gradient would test most steam engines, especially if the train had a dead start from Sheepbridge Station. To work a train up this incline with a Beyer-Garratt type locomotive and 43 wagons of coal would bring the best or worst out of any fireman. Providing that a fireman was prepared to graft, most Beyer-Garratts would respond, and sufficient steam pressure could usually be maintained. Tackling the bank, one day, I was firing for an ex-Keighley driver. The old chap has passed on now, but in his day he was a fine engineman. He was pretty 'new' to Beyer-Garratts and had confessed that he had not driven many of them.

No. 7968 had just returned from Derby Workshops; she looked a picture in her new coat of paint, and her engine number stood out clearly on the tank sides. We approached Hasland Shed with the Beyer-Garratt and a full load of slack, heading for Dronfield Bank. Passing the shed, the lads gave us the thumbs up sign; weren't we lucky to have such a tip-top locomotive. On leaving Tapton Junction we had a good run at the bank, and in the firebox there was a fair amount of fire and coal. The driver quickly opened up and put the regulator right over with the lever up. The sparks were beginning to fly from the chimney and, rolling up my sleeves, I continued to hurl as much coal as possible through the fire hole opening. Quickly closing the fire hole door, I cracked up a very heavy piece of coal with the coal pick, then opening the door again resumed my heavy shovelling. Instead of the Beyer-Garratts steam pressure rising, the finger of the pressure gauge faltered, and hovered between 170 to 180p.s.i. A Beyer-Garratt's blowing off pressure was 190p.s.i. so we had already lost ground. By now I was getting desperate as I knew that as yet I had not put the injector on. Water would soon be showing in the boiler gauge glass, and it was imperative that I should keep it at a good level. Heaving huge lumps of coal into the firebox, I battled on. Sweat was dripping off my forehead; the tension of not being able to maintain full steam adding to my nervousness.

Old Edgar was looking rather perplexed; he had faith in my firing ability, had seen that we got off to a good start, had a spanking new engine but, by now, were not getting proper results. Taking off his jacket and looking out to ensure that all signals were for go, he reached for the spare shovel. Between us, right and left-handed, we alternately kept shovelling away. There appeared to be no waste of steam at the glands, etc.; this was our saviour. We worked the injector in short sessions, and the boiler water level was just holding up.

Battling on up the bank we could hardly believe our eyes, we were burning coal by the barrowful; this was certainly a trip to remember and we would be lucky if we could keep going. In sheer desperation we grafted in our efforts to maintain sufficient steam. Edgar was a stout man and I could smell the perspiration on him. I couldn't blame him for this, and was more than grateful for his continued assistance. If he had not assisted we surely would have had to stop at Unstone or Dronfield for a 'blow up', and things were no better on the rest of the journey. As soon as Edgar showed the Beyer-Garratt plenty of regulator she didn't like it, and refused to steam well. Through the tunnel at Bradway, after my mate had shut down, I had the chance to get more water into the boiler, and prepare for the further challenge of the long Dore and Totley Tunnel. We were having a clear run and, as the engine was belting up to the tunnel mouth, it was again a two shovel operation.

Entering the tunnel my mate sat down and held on to the regulator. He was preparing himself for engine slipping which always seemed to happen in those dark places. Sparks as big as golf balls were hitting the tunnel roof top, and the noise was deafening. We struggled along and were thankful that we were able to keep on going. This was certainly one place where we had no desire to come to grief. After what seemed an eternity, we finally arrived at the Hathersage end of the tunnel, and my mate was able to shut down steam and let the train freewheel down to Hathersage Station where we could fill up the engine's water tanks.

Stopping at the water column my mate shouted out, 'leave this to me Den, and you go and cram some coal into that firebox'! I threw lumps of coal in at will and was really giving the Beyer-Garratt something to chew on. Alas, it was the same story, she just refused to steam freely. We stopped at Normans Bank for a 'blow up', and injected more water into the boiler. Before setting off, Edgar filled our water bottles from a small stream that was trickling out of the rock face by the side of the railway. This water was icy cold and crystal clear. I am sure that both of us lost pounds in weight on that journey as sweat had simply poured off us. We finally made it into Cowburn Tunnel and it was with glorious relief that Edgar shut down the regulator and we started to freewheel towards Chinley. Our water bottles were again empty and, licking our parched lips, we both could hardly wait to get to a water tap. I brewed up some fresh tea in the sidings at Gowholes and, after consuming some of our sandwiches and savouring the tea, we departed for home with a train of 43 empty wagons.

On our return we were stopped several times up the bank by signals, so we were able to jog along without much difficulty. We enjoyed the long run down the high hills from Edale, and gratefully breathed in the fresh mountain air.

Arriving finally at the depot at Hasland, we left the Beyer-Garratt in the slip road for engine disposal. My mate reported 'engine not steaming' and this caused a few eyebrows to be raised. However, the foreman fitter got news of this and was quick to explain the reasons for our engine not steaming well, and why we had burned about 8 tons of coal on a journey of less than 40 miles each way. He said that the blast pipe should have been fitted with a ring inside it before leaving the workshops. It was decided that the engine should be sent to Toton, and the operation would be carried out in their workshops. We had No. 7968 on later trips and she behaved perfectly.

In spite of the heavy work involved, I always had a strong affection for the

Beyer-Garratt locomotives. We had a fair proportion of them booked to Hasland, and therefore got used to them.

A brief description of the coaling-up and watering procedure for the Beyer-Garratts is of interest. On top of the huge rotary type coal drum there were three sets of doors, these were of the double-hinged type and, when fully opened, allowed us plenty of room to be able to tip coal inside the drum. When these doors were closed, they were securely fastened by safety cotters with locking pins. It was imperative that the doors were properly fastened as the coal drums were rotary, and firemen turned them in the course of their duty. After shovelling into a Beyer-Garratt coal drum, a fireman would close the steel doors, release the bottom locking pin, open the steam supply on the boiler front, and operate a steam valve. Steam would drive a donkey engine which, in turn, would cause the coal drum to rotate. Inside the drum were large baffle plates, and these induced coal to fall to the front section of the coal drum. It operated like a large screw. Shutting down the steam supply and securely fastening the drum with the locking pin a fireman could then open the doors and coal would be readily available. This was far better than a tender type engine where a fireman would have to go into the tender and, with his shovel and coal pick, pull coal forward. The water arrangement consisted of a large water tank unit at the front end of the engine, and another water tank at the rear under the coal bunker. When tanking up, water would fill both tanks simultaneously. Only once can I remember something going wrong. There must have been a blockage between the two units, and we noticed that the gauge at the side of the coal drum was not registering, and this gave us the clue. We later reported the blockage and the fitters dealt with it.

Derailments often occurred on railway premises and a lot of these were 'covered up' so nobody was any wiser. Others of course were more 'out in the open' and were noticed.

One such time I was driver on the Sunday pilotman's engine. He was responsible for single line working between Clay Cross Junction, the tunnel, and Stretton. We were inside the old dead end at Stretton with a tank engine, when the signalman called us out on to the main line. This old section had wooden pegs driven into the 'chairs' to keep the rails secured to the old wooden sleepers. These must have been rotten, because as the solid 0-6-0 locomotive moved along, it pushed the rail slightly aside, and the engine became derailed. I was lucky, on this occasion, to find suitable timbers; old sleepers and the like, to wedge under the flanges of the engine wheels. With care and good fortune we got the engine back on to the right lines. I was pleased to see that a few days later that particular section of line was completely renewed with the modern type of rail materials.

Another time, I was not so fortunate. Backing into the carriage sidings at Hollis Lane, our passenger engine split the points and dropped off the rails; engine wheels, tender and all. Unfortunately for me, this time it was a steam-crane job, and I had to request another engine before we could continue with our passenger train to Nottingham.

The most remarkable instance of a derailment that I remember was at Holmewood Colliery. My mate was a rather stout old fellow who demonstrated to me how to keep calm when something went wrong. We were propelling wagons down to the colliery when the first six or seven became derailed. Old Bill surveyed the situation, then passed these casual remarks.

'Well mate, they've come off — let's see if they want to get on again'. Putting the engine in foregear he opened the regulator and the wagons behind us rolled, jumped and finally landed safely back on to the rails. Mind you, circumstances were just right as we were derailed between two other sets of lines. I suppose we must have left a few broken chairs and split wooden slippers in our wake, but the intended job had been done. Cheerfully sucking on his tobacco pipe, my mate sat aloft with a look of contentment all over his face.

On an afternoon trip to Wellingborough, we left Clay Cross Sidings with a Beyer-Garratt and 80 empty steel-sided iron-ore wagons. After putting these off in the sidings at Ashwell, in Rutland, we proceeded, light engine and guard, on our way to Wellingborough. We were coal bunker first and, as we rolled along, small particles of coal dust were still blowing into the cab windows from the ledges on the bunker side frames. These bits could be a nuisance, and we usually endeavoured to move the fire irons before setting off on a journey and clean these ledges down. However, in the course of our journey the greater part of small coal was lying by the lineside along the way, having been blown off by cross winds or by the vibration of our engine.

We passed Oakham and Manton stations, had passed through Glaston Tunnel, and were fast approaching the long Welland Viaduct at Harringworth; this had 82 arches which spanned the wide valley below. The viaduct looked a very impressive, but almost, awesome sight and was often shrouded in mist. It looked a clumsy sort of structure and I was told that the men who made it were indiscriminate in the use of red and blue brick.

This particular day, at about 8.00p.m., the sky was getting dark and the viaduct in front of us presented an eerie sight. I was reflecting on this when suddenly, without any warning, the Beyer-Garratt set up a terrific shudder. We were by now on the viaduct itself, and could see the lights from the cottages below. The unusual banging noise from the engine got louder, and it was as if the Beyer-Garratt also thought this place was eerie and was reluctant to pass over it.

'Bloody hell'!, I heard my mate shout, 'we are off the road'. He quickly closed the partially open regulator and let the engine slowly come to a standstill, using the brake as quickly as he could. The giant locomotive seemed to lurch from side to side. Old Cecil shouted, 'you get down that side, Den — I'll have a look at the other'. Nervously, I climbed down the steel steps from the Beyer-Garratt's cab, and was about to shine my treasured cycle lamp to see what was amiss, when the viaduct started to shake. It was almost as if the place was haunted. The shaking increased, but it wasn't a ghost that was responsible but an express train that was roaring towards us on the opposite line (the 'down' line). It was hurtling down the bank on its way from Corby Tunnel, and the driver was just giving it full throttle. Sparks could be seen flying out of the express engine's chimney and these were cascading like fireworks into the valley below.

I dared not run back to the protection of the cab and was reluctant to try to get to the front or rear of our engine. Instead, I elected to press my back firmly against the Beyer-Garratt framing and motions, holding tightly to one of the connecting links. Water from the leading tank under the coal bunker was trickling down my face and neck, but I dared not move. In seconds, the express was rocketing past us, kicking up bits of ballast on its way, I could feel

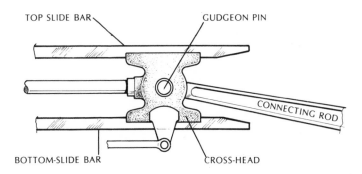

TOP SLIDE BAR GUDGEON PIN

CONNECTING ROD

BOTTOM-SLIDE BAR CROSS-HEAD

With reference to the Beyer-Garratt breaking down on Harringworth Viaduct, here is a sketch of a gudgeon pin's position.

the heat from the giant locomotive as it charged by, and the noise was deafening. The draught it created pulled at my overalls, and this continued until the engine and coaches had passed. It was soon over, and I was relieved to see the red tail lamps of the guard's coach as the train disappeared round the bend into Seaton Tunnel.

Pulling myself together, and with limbs shaking, I tentatively shone my lamp around the sleepers and the engine motions. Everything seemed to be in order except for that steady trickle of water from the tank above me. Going round to the rear of the engine I noticed my mate, almost with his head inside the motions, shining his lamp up and down. 'Are you alright, Den'? he shouted. 'Not bad' I replied, 'but I'm glad that bloody thing has passed by'. 'Just look at this lot', my mate continued, and, following his gaze in the torchlight, I could hardly believe my eyes. Some of the rods were bent and the heavy long connecting rod was out of the crosshead. The gudgeon pin was missing and all we could see was the brass inside the crosshead. 'What a bloody place to come to grief', my mate exclaimed frustratingly. 'Let's thank our lucky stars', I exclaimed, 'we could have been in Glaston Tunnel back there'. 'I suppose we have got to count our blessings', my mate retorted, 'just think, Den, if the connecting rod had come uncoupled at the other side and the bottom slide bar had broken, we might even have got pushed over the side of the viaduct'. This was a terrifying thought, a bit melodramatic I suppose, but there wasn't a lot of room from the track to the low wall on top of the viaduct. Sensibly, my mate asked me to protect our disabled engine, I hurriedly climbed back into the engine cab and took the can of detonators out of the cupboard. Quickly, I ran, stumbling back down the line, occasionally slipping on the greasy sleepers. I clipped a detonator on the rail at a reasonable quarter mile distance, then another at a half mile. Looking back over my shoulder I could

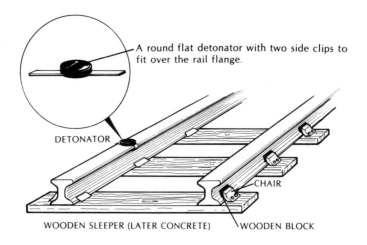

A round flat detonator with two side clips to fit over the rail flange.

DETONATOR

CHAIR

WOODEN SLEEPER (LATER CONCRETE)   WOODEN BLOCK

Platelayers checked the rails daily and, if wooden blocks had moved or were missing, these would be hammered back into position by the platelayers. Modern present day tracks have a different arrangement.

A sketch of a section of track and the fixing of detonators.

see the 'up' main line signal with its green light shining through the gloom. I thought, 'good God' — if anything comes behind us my poor old mate back there is a sitting duck. This spurred me on and at about the three-quarter mile distance I placed three detonators at ten yard intervals.

By now I was at the mouth of the short Seaton Tunnel, so, walking through, I placed a further three detonators 10yds. apart at the end of the tunnel. Feeling that my mate and the Beyer-Garratt were sufficiently protected, I took a few minutes to get my breath back. My mate wasn't the type to give up easily, so I made my way back to our disabled locomotive to give him as much assistance as I could. Hurrying back, and shining my light on to the permanent way, I couldn't believe my luck when I came across the gudgeon pin, and also the nut that had come off the end. The end part of the gudgeon pin had broken off, allowing the whole lot to become uncoupled — unfortunately, I couldn't find the collar. I showed my mate the gudgeon pin and he excitedly exclaimed, 'you know Den, we might get off this bloody viaduct after all'.

He had been back in the engine cab and with the brake on had gently opened the regulator and the heavy connecting rod had ultimately been forced back into the crosshead. Luck was now on our side, and to the rear of the crosshead there was a space between the wheel spokes. My mate reached over and, with great effort, managed to push the weighty pin back into position with the flanged end nearest the wheel. Our dilemma was that, with the collar missing, the pin would work out again, but here was an instance of quick thinking. My driver broke a wooden block out of the chair that holds the rails in position, and inserted the pieces around the nut, like wedges, and turning round said, 'now then, sonny boy, let's see what we can do'. Cautiously we moved along, a wheel revolution, or two, at a time, and finally reached Harringworth signal box, and the safety of the sidings. My arms had ached throughout this whole tedious operation as I had to continually keep knocking the wedges back into position with the coal pick. Cis deserved a medal for his efforts and patience under such trying conditions; lesser men would have given up long before.

Safely clear of the main line, trains were again allowed to proceed on the 'up' line. Fortunately, the first one was a light engine. The driver of this had been told by phone where to expect detonators and had cautiously 'cracked them off' as he came into the Harringworth section. A breakdown train arrived with fitters from Kettering and they fully stripped down the damaged motions, and finally towed the Beyer-Garratt to the engine shed with the breakdown engine. We were relieved, and went on another train to Wellingborough Barracks to lodge.

There is a rule on the railway which says that any light waved violently denotes danger. Believe me, if anything had approached me as I hastened down the line on that unforgettable occasion, I would certainly have carried out those instructions with some fervour.

Chapter Seven

AIR ATTACKS ON YORK

Looking back on our earlier experience when we came so close to being really 'caught up' in the Sheffield blitz, there is another similar incident. Again we must have had our 'Guardian Angel' with us.

This particular day we were assigned to take a train of ironstone to York. On these trips we mostly had Beyer-Garratts, Class 8 freights, Class 9 freights or Austerity-type engines. On this occasion it was different, and we had a Midland 0-8-0 Class 7 freight. The York run from Swinton consisted of a series of ups and downs — Frickley Bank, Moorthorpe Bank, and so on. It was very interesting to watch my mate George keenly observe all the signals. As we rolled down one bank with the brake partially applied, and the train under his control, he would be hoping for the distant signals to change to the clear position, then he would allow the train couplings to stretch out and, giving the engine a steady increase of regulator, with the lever well up, would literally thunder the train through the dip and, therefore, have a good run at the bank in front of us. Using this technique, we were half-way up the next bank before our engine really felt the heavy weight behind it. I would endeavour to try and ensure that my mate had a full head of steam on these occasions.

It could be rather startling sometimes, when, on arriving at the summit of Moorthorpe Bank, we would encounter sudden cross winds. The side doors might be blown open by the force of the wind, and coal on the footplate could be sent scuttling on to the lineside. Bearing in mind that the train had come from Wellingborough and the coal was low on the tender, you can imagine that we would now be burning a lot of the smaller, crushed, stuff. At times, the coal would be blown off the shovel if the fireman was firing the engine at that particular spot. The trip on the Class 7 freight was no exception, and I lost a few shovelfuls of slack when I was caught unawares.

The few experiences I had on this class of engine were good ones, and if I did have a complaint, it would be that I felt the engine cabs were too short for an engine of that size. The fireboxes were rather long, and I thought that if the cab had been as roomy as a Class 8 freight, for instance, it would have made firing much easier. It was a lot better for a fireman when he was able to move about and flex his muscles; he would then confidently be able to 'hear' the coal 'thud' as it hit the front end of the long box.

On this trip things were going well, and it wasn't long before we were on the easy stretch of line, and were soon about to pass Sherburn and Church Fenton Airfield; this is where the excitement I mentioned earlier was about to begin.

It was again a nice clear, crisp, moonlit night. George was now only using a breath of steam in the cylinders to keep the train moving along. We had been stopped down the line and told that we were on air raid warning red. It wasn't always possible to hear the sirens on the footplates, so the procedure was that, at the first opportunity, the signalman would inform us about it. Looking up to the sky old George shouted out, 'bloody hell! there is a plane diving down on us'. This was war at its most serious. Again the plane flew right over us and could easily have been in a position to blow us to 'kingdom come'. Fortunately for us I am convinced that this one was only acting as a pathfinder. He could have strafed us with his machine guns, but perhaps did not want to give away his presence too soon. Flying just above us for that split second he suddenly veered off and dropped flares around one of the airfields. As these hit the ground they turned to a green sort of light and, like the roman candle type of firework, the flames rose to about 6 or 7ft. in no time at all. We could see people running about, attempting to stamp out these deadly tell-tales. Men appeared to be using brooms and shovels, and no doubt would soon be dousing the flares with water. I reflected 'Oh no, not Sheffield again', and I am sure that my mate was sharing my sentiments. He opened up the regulator and shouted, 'bloody hell, let's get away from here'. Fortunately, for us, all signals were for a clear run, and we were soon moving along at a fair old trot.

I was completely caught up in the atmosphere and grabbed for the shovel to start firing the engine. My usually placid mate, George, turned on me and screamed 'bugger the shovel, keep those bloody fire hole doors shut'. He surely must have realised that the enemy had seen us, open fire doors or not, but he was in no mood to give away any advantage. We had a fairly decent depth of fire still in the firebox and, in spite of my discontinued firing, the steam pressure held up well. By now we were fast approaching a distant signal at caution, so my mate had to shut down and quickly get the heavy train under control. The train was brought to a standstill on the outskirts of York and, as we stood there, we could hear aeroplanes overhead. These sounded much heavier than the first one and, over in the distance, we thought that we heard bombs being dropped. The ground staff at the airfields back down the line must have done a speedy job in extinguishing the flares. I cannot recall hearing any stories about damage to their premises on that occasion. Anyway, York had a let-off that night, and no bombs were dropped over the city. I don't suppose any bomber crews took their heavy loads back home with them after these sort of raids so, sadly, some other town or village may have had to suffer their wrath. This was a far different story from the one an old mate of mine related to me.

He too was at York in similar circumstances, but it was a Tuesday evening, 28th April 1942. German bombers came in waves from the direction of the East Coast; they seemed intent on destroying York Station that night, as bombs were falling heavily in that part of the city. York had been invaded before, he said, but never like this — the early Romans could hardly have possessed such devastating weapons. A signal box was hit, an express train was set on fire, and sections of the goods yards were ablaze. Glass from the huge oval station roof was crashing all around. My mate said he saw a huge North Eastern locomotive lying twisted on its side near to the engine shed. I have personally seen photographs of this and they clearly showed the engine nameplate *Sir Ralph Wedgwood*. Like Sheffield, the fires were so intense that they only helped to brighten up the sky for the endless waves of enemy bombers. This, plus the light from the moon, was again a bomb-aimers field day. If 'Jerry' had succeeded on this mission in April 1942, he would surely have crippled a vital part of the East Coast network.

York was the main centre for trains to the East Coast and the convoy ships which would be waiting for their vital supplies, and our ironstone trains would be stopped from reaching the steelworks in the Middlesborough area. Fortunately, for all concerned, this didn't happen, and once again the great British spirit was in evidence.

Men and women worked endlessly round the clock in their efforts to help the injured, remove the debris, and try to restore sanity to the crippled City of York. The flow of vital supplies to the ports was able to proceed, but a great price was paid. More than seventy people were killed, and thousands of house owners suffered loss or damage to their property. It was to be years before the station at York would look the same again.

We lodged in private lodgings on the York runs and, on a lighter note, I well remember the dear old lady who put us up. She was the fussy type and always insisted on frying our breakfast for us. This was all very well, but she did have a nasty habit of dropping our sausages on the kitchen floor, 'dusting' them on her pinafore, and returning them back to the frying pan.

Chapter Eight

DRIVER TRAINING AND DRIVING DUTIES

Turning up for duty at Hasland the foreman told me that I was to be passed for a driver the following day. 'You do not give people much notice do you', I remarked. Then the foreman said that the inspector had just failed a man and I was to have an examination in his place. This didn't do my spirits any good and when I arrived home I poured out the story to my wife. 'If you don't know enough now for the railway inspector, you never will', she said. She was reflecting on the fact that she had been my question master for months. I was grateful to her for taking time and patience to ask me questions from the railway black book and red rule book; the black book covering the working of engines. There was a saying that railwaymen's wives used to place the egg cups on the table, one at quarter, one at a half and three at three-quarters (remember the protection rules).

The time arrived for me to meet Inspector Summers from Sheffield. Our interview was to be in the breakdown coach which was standing in the back sidings at Hasland. The idea was that this place was quiet and comfortable, and we would not be disturbed. I was asked all sorts of questions, both on Rules and Regulations, and also on the working and function of a locomotive. We adjourned later for lunch and then had a further session. I cannot remember all those technical details now, and do not intend to try, but I will always remember two things. The first took me completely by surprise because of its simplicity. The inspector asked, 'what is oil for?' I answered, 'to eliminate friction'. He looked hard at me and again asked. 'Tell me what oil is for in one word'. Pausing, I thought hard and then said, 'to separate'. The inspector laughed and said 'that's right lad; oil is used to separate'. This was something to remember, and when working locomotives try at all times to 'separate' metal surfaces with oil from our faithful oilcan.

The second small question I remember was being asked what I knew about the vacuum brake. 'What is the secret of the vacuum brake on the coaches?' the Inspector asked. 'The ball valve at the bottom of the cylinder', I replied. 'Correct' said the Inspector. 'It's like a policeman on duty isn't it'. What an apt description, and I have remembered it to this day. When the ejector valve was opened, steam passed up the chimney, thus drawing all the air from the train pipe and connections. On application of the brake, air was admitted to the bottom of the cylinder. The ball valve did the rest; like a policeman, it 'regulated' the flow of air. Once the ball valve was thrown on to its face, air couldn't get to the top of the piston and rushed to the bottom and, 'Bob's your uncle'. When anyone pulled the communication cord, this had the same effect. Air would be admitted into the train pipe and, therefore, partially applied the brakes.

The following day, after the questions and answers on Rules and Regulations, etc., the Inspector took me out on to the 'road'. I was required to drive a passenger train to Trent Station and a goods train on the return journey. Meeting the Inspector on Chesterfield Station platform in the morning, we waited until a passenger train stopped at the south end. This turned out to be a stopping passenger train which would call at all stations to Trent. The regular driver was requested to go into the coaches, and it was explained to his fireman that I was to undergo a driving test. I should mention that I had fired for some really good drivers on passenger work, who had let me do a lot of driving for them. With their teaching in mind, and all their advice, I felt pretty confident. I was on home ground and knew almost every yard of that particular stretch of railway. Setting off, we were soon approaching Clay Cross Station, which would be our first stop. Applying the vacuum brake, I felt it get hold of the coaches and, after a decent application, the train coasted into the station, with the brake literally 'coming off'. This saved snatching the coaches and inconveniencing passengers by stopping too quickly. The engine chimney was clear of the station walkover and so the smoke was not finding its way into the station buildings. 'You have done that before, haven't you?' remarked the Inspector. This small remark gave me confidence. The next stop was Doe Hill, a tricky little station with a platform that could just accommodate four coaches, then Westhouses Station and Alfreton. We had a 4P Compound 4-4-0, and were really flying towards Alfreton. 'Stop the engine with the chimney clear of the bridge', instructed the Inspector. This was to avoid smoke or steam causing a nuisance to anyone crossing the bridge. Again the operation turned out to be successful and the Inspector quipped, 'it's like shelling peas, isn't it?' After a remark like that I knew that things were going alright. We stopped at all stations down the Erewash Valley and finally arrived at Trent Station. The Compound was handed back to the Millhouses driver and we waved them a cheery 'good morning'.

There was a Beyer-Garratt approaching on the 'down' line with a train of iron-ore wagons. This consisted of about 50 trucks, fully loaded, and would be a heavy train. 'How would you like to have a go on this one?' the Inspector asked. I don't suppose there was any alternative, really, but in my heart of hearts I knew that I could cope. After all, we had been brought up with the Beyer-Garratts.

We set off towards Toton and the Erewash Valley again, and the Inspector picked up the shovel and commenced firing. He still had his heavy black coat and bowler hat on, but even so, was showing me that he had done all this before. On the heavier part of the line, he discarded his hat and coat and continued to fire the engine like an old hand. When she was popping off at the safety valves he washed his hands in the bucket, sat down on the fireman's seat, and told the lad, 'right son, now you have a go'. Eventually we arrived at our destination, applying the handbrake, putting the lever out of gear and opening the cylinder cocks, I climbed down the steps of the engine cab. The Inspector followed me and, as I walked round the giant locomotive, he waited for my remarks. With the back of my hand I was touching the bearings to check if any were running hot, and, at the same time, was looking for anything that might be wrong with the workings of the engine. The Inspector was casting an eagle eye, and I realised that I must not miss anything. The brake blocks were wearing, there was a leak on the rear water tank, and a couple of springs had moved in their hangers. I shouted to the fireman to apply first the front and then the rear sanders. A couple of these were blocked with pebbles, but otherwise the engine appeared to be in decent condition. By now the train driver had walked up from the guard's van where, no doubt, he had been having a 'kip'. Passing the above information to him, and thanking him, the Inspector and I walked on to Chesterfield Station platform. This is where it had all begun earlier that day, so what was to be Mr. Summers' verdict?

The Inspector shook me by the hand, said 'well done lad' and then these unforgettable words. 'When you get home, tell your wife that she will be sleeping with an engine driver tonight'. 'Be a good lad', the Inspector concluded, 'and try to keep out of trouble for six months'. He would be responsible for me for that period. Well, I didn't let him down, and will always be grateful to him and remember him as a perfect gentleman. I had earlier attended his lectures at Sheffield and to hear him talk about locomotives was a revelation. He always backed up his statements with his own drawings, and these were excellent.

I was soon to get my first driving trips, and these early ones were mainly local and would be with tank engines, Class 3 freights, Class 4 freights, 8Fs and Beyer-Garratts. On my sixth trip I experienced my first real test. I was soon to realise that driving on one's own was a different kettle of fish to driving for somebody else who would take all responsibility. I was out of the cradle now, and all major decisions were to be mine. It was about 5p.m. and the foreman at our depot informed me that I was to assist an express train to Sheffield. There was a Class 2 passenger engine, fully prepared, standing in the shed yard. The express would be due in about half an hour, and we were to couple-up engines at the Hasland 'down' home main line. Quickly checking the state of the engine fire, and noticing that the water level was alright, I started to build up a good heavy fire; I was making sure that, on my first express driving trip, I would at least get a good start.

Piling coal into the box, I didn't let up until I felt confident that the firebox was really heavily lined. By now the express train was approaching, so leaving the shed with our assisting engine we went out on to the main line. My fireman had never coupled up two locomotives in this situation, so after backing up to the express engine and ensuring both engine buffers were well pressed up, I decided to do the job myself. The train engine fireman was removing his engine's headlamps, and told me that they were having trouble maintaining steam. He said that the train consisted of ten coaches so that would be about 310 tons. If the reader has ever seen two steam locomotives being coupled together, he will realise that it could be a tricky operation. After tightening the screw coupling to ensure both engine buffers were firmly together, the fireman would couple up the brake vacuum hoses. These had hook-shaped lugs at the end, were strong and thick, but flexible, and needed a strong wrist action to make sure that they fitted together properly. As with anything else, there was a knack of doing this, and only practice could help a fireman to do it successfully. With the engine firmly coupled, the signal was lowered and we set off on our journey to Sheffield. This was to be the first stop, so would be an advantage to me. Most express trains were scheduled to stop at Chesterfield, but on this particular trip we would be able to have a good run right through and get a better start at Dronfield Bank. All signals were clear, and we were really travelling down towards Tapton Junction. I will always remember that trip — I had to give the Class 2 a lot of regulator to ensure that we really assisted the flagging locomotive behind us. We probably 'lost' some time, but at last finally reached the summit of the bank at Bradway Tunnel. Our previously-prepared heavy fire had been a godsend to us, and the engine had steamed perfectly. My young mate was firmly seated in the corner and I had done the firing myself. Starting to pick up speed on the downward part of Bradway Tunnel I shouted to my mate to hang on to the injector handle and stay in that corner. The noise was deafening in the tunnel as the two engines pounded away. Then, after a short distance into the tunnel, we both shut down steam. We were now on the downhill part, and our speed was increasing. The whole weight of two engines and ten coaches was picking up speed as they freewheeled down to Sheffield. Keeping a good look-out for the distant signal for Heeley Carriage Sidings, I had let the train continue to pick up speed. Whenever this particular signal was at 'caution', drivers had to quickly make their minds up and give the brake a good application so that they could stop at the signals for Heeley Carriage Sidings. All signals were at 'go' and, after passing the sidings, I was slowly applying the brake to really get the speed down and prepare for a gentler run into Sheffield Station. It was rather a unique set up of lines just before entering Sheffield (Midland) Station. After Heeley Station, the trains on the left-hand main lines would go straight on, but trains on the right-hand main lines would go under the ground through a series of tunnels, and come out of these almost side by side with the other main line. We travelled under the tunnels and emerged and, with all signals clear, slowly drew into No. 1 platform at Sheffield. Stopping the train so that the rear engine could take water, we uncoupled and went on to the turntable to prepare for a return trip south again.

This first express trip of mine was only just over 12 miles, but on that particular section it had everything — a gradient to tackle and a really fast run down the other side and a stop at a water crane with an express; this could sometimes be tricky. I think that we had given my young mate quite a scare, but it would be something he too would remember from his first main line trip.

Ringing up Control we were instructed to assist an express to Derby — first stop Chesterfield. Again I fired and drove our engine the whole of the way, and the train driver must have thought that this was my busy day. No doubt he had done the same thing many times himself. He would see our antics as we had a lower type tender, and he would easily see over it from his larger type engine cab. On our return journey we had a good trip, kept time, and eventually coasted into Derby Station, again proceeding to the outside turntable to prepare for further work home. There were no further trains requiring assistance, so we made our way home with the light engine. This was a good opportunity for my mate to 'feel his feet', as I rather suspected that they must have shaken a little. It was about as much as he could manage, and I felt that he would need a lot more experience before being competent to fire on main line goods trains or passenger workings.

I was to get many more assisting trips on longer distances and really looked forward to them. To be in control of a train with the continuous brake system was far better than working a loose-coupled train; then, a driver only had the steam brake on his engine and tender to rely on, and the more trips we got the

Plate 33: Beyer-Garratt No. 47971 rolls round the curve in the cutting at Dore & Totley with a mineral train for the Gowholes sidings on 25 July 1953. They would soon be on the upward climb to the long Dore & Totley tunnel.

B. Goodlad

Plate 34: A view of Hasland Shed without a roof as weeds take over the ashpits. On the turntable is an Hughes-Fowler Class 4, No. 43090, and in the foreground on the straight pit is Stanier Class 5, No. 45006. The sand-house chimney is still visible in the background.

C. Machin

Plate 35: Another Beyer-Garratt, No. 47973, in the shed yard at Hasland. The coal bunker front an_ middle doors can be seen fully open after the engine had come from under the coaling plant in th background. The round surfaces in the foreground were preparations for the installation of storag tanks for oil-burning locomotives.

*Gordon Colta_*

Plate 36: An LMS 'Jubilee' Class, No. 45660, leaving Dore & Totley at Rooke, with an 'up' slow passenge_ train to Dore, on 9 May 1953.

*B. Goodla_*

Plate 37: An elevated view of Dore & Totley Station. An 8F freight engine, No. 48314, propels a guards van in the Dore West direction, whilst to the right No. 45285 hauls a special St. Pancras express passenger.

B. Goodlad

Plate 38: A Class 7F 0-8-0, No. 49598, at Mirfield on 21 April 1956, similar to the one described on the trip to York when enemy aircraft were flying overhead.

B. Goodlad

Plate 39: The last Beyer-Garratt locomotive in service was No. 47994, pictured in Crewe Works Yard c Sunday, 30 March 1958. Its final home, prior to withdrawal was Hasland, and its last run was from Toto to Hasland on Friday, 28 February 1958. It then left Hasland Shed, light engine, for Crewe Works 7.30 a.m. on Friday, 14 March 1958, to arrive at Crewe on Saturday, 15 March 1958. Its offici withdrawal date was 29 March 1958. It was built by Beyer Peacock & Co. Ltd., Gorton, Manchester, 1930, and was originally numbered 4994, being renumbered 7994 in April 1939. I was the driver on March 1958 and my fireman was Norman Wildgoose. We were relieved at Derby Station by a Derb crew as we were not familiar with the LNWR line from Stenson Junction.

Courtesy Chesterfield Librar

Plate 40: LNER Class A4 locomotive, No. 4469 *Sir Ralph Wedgwood* after being damaged in the air ra on York Station on 29 April 1942.

National Railway Museum, Yo

Plate 41: Compound 4-4-0, No. 41154, passing Dore & Totley West Junction with a four-coach, slow passenger train for Chinley, on 4 July 1953.

B. Goodlad

Plate 42: The scene of devastation at York Station after the air raid on 29 April 1942.

National Railway Museum, York

Plate 43: A Beyer-Garratt, No. 47990, leaving Barrow Hill Shed Sidings on the way to coal up.

B. Handfo

Plate 44: No. 40691, Class 2P stands with 'light engine' headlamp code on coaches at Nottingha Station. This locomotive, as detailed in the text, kicked up sparks into the cab whilst on a run fr Sheffield to Derby, due to the spring hangers being out of balance.

P. Waym

Plate 45: The water column on the turntable road at Gowholes, near Chinley. This 1956 view shows the fireman struggling to haul up the heavy leather water bag from the column. Perhaps his mate had gone to mash the tea.

J. Birkes

Plate 46: Freezing conditions in the Staveley area. Steam from an 8F engine is being used to clear snow and ice from points after a heavy snowfall.

B. Chapman

Plate 47: A Class 4F, No. 44271, at Buxton on 8 January 1956, showing the stout equipment needed t tackle the heavy snow falls which fell to great depths in the bleak Derbyshire district in wintertime

B. Goodla

Plate 48: A 5XP 'Patriot' Class 4-6-0 locomotive passes Dronfield colliery sidings on the 'down' main li with an express passenger train.

B. Chapma

Plate 49: Beyer-Garratt, No. 47998, passes Tapton Junction on the 'down' line with a heavy goods train on 28 August 1954. Note the straight coal bunker. Neither 47998 nor 47999 were fitted with rotary coal drums.

B. Goodlad

Plate 50: A Black Five 4-6-0, No. 44816, approaches Tapton Junction on the 'down' goods line.

C. Machin

Plate 51: Two BR Standard locomotives, a freight 2-10-0, No. 92057, and a Class 5, 4-6-0 mixed traffi
engine, race south to Clay Cross after passing Avenue Sidings.

C. Mach

Plate 52: The fireman breaks up coal in the tender of an 'Austerity' on the turntable road at Gowhol
Sidings. We tanked up with water here on many occasions.

B. Chapma

Plate 53: In October 1956, Beyer-Garratt No. 47972 hauls a heavy mineral train up Dronfield Bank. Note the leaking steam from the badly packed glands, etc. It was on this bank where we struggled with No. 47968 and finished up emptying the coal bunker on our return.

J. Birkes

Plate 54: A Hasland 2P engine, No. 40502, approaches Chesterfield from Tapton Junction with an express from Sheffield.

B. Goodlad

Plate 55: No. 45712 *Victory* on a 'down' express near Whitmore troughs in August 1955. This picture shows the length of water troughs necessary for the driver to be able to pick up a sufficient supply of water.

B. Goodlad

Plate 56: Stanier 'Jubilee' No. 45589 racing out of the 88 yard long Broomhouse tunnel on the fast downward run to Sheepbridge, Tapton and Chesterfield with an express parcels train. This tunnel is now removed and is just a railway cutting with a small footbridge over it.

B. Handford

Plate 57: An 'Austerity', No. 90427, on a Class B goods train, at Horns Bridge on the 'up' goods line. The Central Railways loop line runs under the Midland line at this point. The crooked spire of the Parish Church of St. Mary and All Saints in Chesterfield is clearly seen in the background.

C. Machin

Plate 58: A busy time in the short 90 yard Totley tunnel. Track relaying is in progress and the ganger is taking an elevated view of the proceedings. Class 8F, No. 4815, is being used to position wagons near to the tunnel opening.

P. Hawkins

Plate 59: Compound engine, No. 41071, pulls out of Sheffield Midland Station heading south on 16 Jul 1955.

B. Goodla

Plate 60: Ladybower Dam in the Derwent Valley. This view gives a good idea of the run up a 'Dam Buster' pilot would have had when practising with the skimming bomb technique. When the dams wer constructed a special railway area was set out near Bamford called Waterboard Sidings; these cope with a lot of heavy materials which were then moved up to the dam site.

G. W. Marti

ate 61: An 8F 2-8-0, No. 48538, at Tapton Junction with a long heavy goods train, passes on the 'up' ods line. An engine and guards van wait at the signals on the 'down' goods line. Another engine and ake van stand in the left hand sidings and the 'down' main line signals are 'all clear' for the old route vards Barrow Hill.

B. Goodlad

ate 62: 'Jubilee', No. 45699 *Galatea*, passes over the short viaduct beyond the 'down' home signal at stone on the Dronfield bank line, with the north bound 'Devonian' express.

B. Chapman

Plate 63: An elevated view of the empty Hasland Shed. This is a far cry from the hustle and bustle earlier days.

C. Mach

Plate 64: A desolute landscape at Hasland after the Shed was demolished. Only the railwaymer cottages remain standing. To the top right of the water column can just be seen the entrance to th wartime air raid shelter, which was buried into the bank side.

C. Mach

higher our wages would be. We needed the equivalent of three years continuous driving to attain the same rate as a fully-fledged driver; a total of 313 trips constituted a full year as we disregarded the 52 Sundays, so that meant 939 trips in all. Many of our trips were in front of the 'Devonian' express at that time. They seemed to make a lot of fuss about her keeping time; I don't really know why.

During the football season there were soccer excursions to be worked, so here we had more chances to get more trips; these may have been only to York, Leeds, Derby, Leicester or Nottingham, but they all counted. On a Derby evening kick-off excursion, we once had a Class 4 freight engine and after I had oiled the engine at the depot and checked all around, my fireman drew my attention to the fact that the tubes in the firebox were leaking — I told him that I had noticed it when I first checked our steam pressure. He seemed to be getting fussy about the situation, and hinted that I ought to ask for another engine. It was getting too near departure time to think about that, and I advised my mate to put some coal into the firebox. Once the temperature rose, the leaking tube ends would soon dry up again; the higher temperature would expand them. We had a good trip and went 'round the houses' to pick up our Derby football supporters.

Instead of the usual straight run through Stretton and Wingfield, we went via Pye Bridge, Ironville and Butterley, returning to the Derby line at Crich Junction for Ambergate. In spite of the earlier leaking tubes, my mate had no difficulty in maintaining steam. However, the leaking tubes were reported when we returned to the shed. Once we reached the ashpit and started to drop the fire, the tubes started to leak again — the temperature had fallen, so they started to contract. I have seen tube plates that were literally pouring with water 'take up' in similar conditions to those to which I have just referred.

One day I was privileged to drive a VIP train. It was a Directors' Special and consisted of just the engine and an observation coach. The engine looked immaculate and had been specially cleaned for this trip. The fellow in charge was sort of 'guard-come-valet', and was in the coach with the Directors. They were sitting at the rear looking through the wide observation windows. The coach seemed to have 'all mod cons' inside, and was fit to live in. The foreman had previously issued me with papers that contained instructions of when and where to go. We called at many of the local collieries and then we were to visit various places en route to Nottingham, including Westhouses and Toton engine sheds. On my instructions I noticed that it showed a three minute stop at Clay Cross Station, but it didn't say for what purpose. When approaching the goods line signals at Clay Cross North Junction we were halted so that an express train could go by on the 'up' main line. When this had cleared the South Junction, our points were pulled up and the signals lowered for us to proceed on to the main line. We were dead on time, so I assumed that this was the three minutes referred to in my notes. The distant signals were in the clear position so, opening the regulator, we set off to our left and on to the Erewash line — next stop Morton. Passing through Clay Cross Station, I waved to the stationmaster who was standing on the platform, and he politely waved back — and continued to wave; I couldn't help but notice how smart the stationmaster appeared — nice dark suit, top hat etc. However, we soon passed him by and, after many stops and what seemed endless handshaking by the VIPs, we finally arrived at Nottingham. The Directors started to disembark, and I was to proceed with the empty coach to a special lay-by near to the carriage sidings. One of the Directors came up to our spotless little Ivatt class engine and presented me with a pound note. 'Well done, old boy' he exclaimed, and then said 'here, have a drink on me'. Then he laughed heartily and, still grinning, said, 'tell me, why didn't you stop the train in Clay Cross Station?' I was speechless, goodness me, of all trains to slip up with, it had to be this one. I felt very embarrassed and immediately thought about the three minutes at Clay Cross. 'Oh, forget it', he said, 'we all had a jolly good laugh at the stationmaster as you passed him by'. 'Didn't he look smart — really, you know, we were expected to shake hands with him'. Looking back I realised that I had ruined the poor old stationmaster's big moment.

We were working a slow passenger train from Nottingham to Chesterfield, stopping at all stations. On leaving Alfreton it was noticed that the finger on the vacuum gauge was going down; at the same time the brakes on the coaches started to drag. Quickly opening the large ejector and putting the regulator right over, I dropped the gear lever down and made for Westhouses Station, which was only minutes away. We suspected that somebody had pulled the communication cord, and so we wanted to get under the protection of signals before we investigated. In cases like these we were taught to try and get clear of tunnels or viaducts if at all possible. When trains did stop in sections, for no apparent reason, passengers sometimes had a nasty habit of trying to get out of the coaches.

Approaching Westhouses Station, the engine was shut down, and the train rolled into the platform. The large ejector was shut off and the brake applied; we came to a standstill. Quickly running back along the platform to tell the guard, I noticed a drunken man struggling out of a carriage door. He was the culprit and it appears that he wanted to alight at Alfreton, was somewhat stupified, and realised that we had passed that station by. Reaching up for the communication cord he had attempted to try and stop us. In incidents such as these it was quite easy to find the coach where the chain had been pulled as there was a butterfly valve at each end of the coach and these were normally in the horizontal position. If the cord was pulled, they were turned to vertical, and the chain in the coach would stay hanging down until the butterfly valves were altered and the chain tightened up again. We left the drunk to make his excuses to the station staff and went on our journey. No doubt he would be fined for his foolishness. Communication cords can, of course, be life savers, and in fact have been used to stop trains when travelling passengers have noticed fires in coaches. Other people who have been ill, or even attacked, on trains have pulled the cords in self defence. It is all a matter of common sense, where and when to use them.

One night, when working a colliery trip with a Class 4 freight engine, we were propelling wagons down an incline into railway sidings; the wagons were stabled in these prior to being lowered down to a colliery. The guard stopped us and, before we realised what was going to happen, he knocked off the wagon coupling from the engine tender hook. We were horrified, as he should have pinned a lot of the wagon brakes down before uncoupling from the engine. Putting on the engine brake we jumped down on to the ballast and, grabbing brake sticks, ran after the wagons. The three of us managed to drop a few brakes but the wagons ran away from us. They hit the buffers at the bottom of the colliery yard and there was coal dust for everybody.

Fortunately, the colliery staff were having their break in the canteen, which was about a quarter of a mile away. Then we did a risky and, maybe, foolish thing which might have got us all into trouble. There was a notice on a post saying 'No Midland engines must pass this post'. Obviously the railway lines in the colliery yard wouldn't be maintained to main line standards and they would also be used by colliery tank engines. Cautiously, we ventured on to these prohibited lines and 'retrieved' the wagons. Trying not to make too much noise we returned them to the railway sidings. This was another lesson learned, and in the future we would ensure that the wagons were securely fastened down before easing on to them.

Whilst still on the subject of colliery yards, we used to admire the way the old tank engine drivers dashed about the colliery yard premises. Their 'steeds' were often tied up with wire and pieces of rope with bits of corrugated iron sheeting sometimes wedged at the side to protect the drivers from bad weather. They used to really dash up and down those creaky old rails. Lots of present day preservation societies seem to treasure their saddle tanks. Often, on today's films, we see them pulling passenger trains, the film producers no doubt using the societies' premises to simulate railway life. I must confess that my memories of those engines are not so good. Often when they were 'clapped out', we had the job of taking them to Derby Workshops for repair. It could be a nightmare sometimes and, after travelling just a few miles, we have had to be shunted off the main line while axleboxes have cooled down. The engines would be taken to 'dead man's lane' at Derby — sounds appropriate, doesn't it? We always took the engines into a dead end with their tenders facing the workshops. There must have been a reason for this, but I never found out what it was. After these little engines were repaired, it was a different story. They looked a picture, and their old colliery drivers welcomed them back lovingly.

Here is an account that is worth recording. On a cattle train from Rotherham (Masboro') to Leicester, our guard noticed from the truck labels that the cattle inside had not been exercised, fed, or watered for a considerable length of time. In some of the trucks a few of the unfortunate beasts were lying on the floorboards and were being trampled on. The train consisted of about 30 trucks, and it wasn't a pleasant sight to see the plight of these animals and hear their plaintive cries; the stench didn't help things either. This guard deserves a medal from the National Society for the Prevention of Cruelty to Animals for his humane and prompt action as he immediately made arrangements for the train to be shunted into some cattle docks so that they received attention. Unfortunately, the nearest docks were in Chesterfield goods yard, about 20 miles or so away. The train was to terminate at Leicester, but this guard felt that the cattle had suffered enough, so he instructed us to go carefully to Chesterfield and shunt inside the sidings when we reached Horns Bridge. Before we left Rotherham, the guard and some shunters prodded the animals who were laid on the floorboards until they got to their feet. Arriving eventually at Chesterfield, we shunted our train into the sidings, but unfortunately the cattle docks only held a few cattle trucks at one time. The guard insisted that each short section should be placed near the docks, and the cattle were allowed to exercise and take water. This process was repeated time and time again, and we were beginning to wonder if the poor animals would have been better to carry on in the first place. We stayed so long in the goods yard that another crew eventually relieved us to take the train to Leicester. This was a long drawn-out process, but it gave a lot of satisfaction to a lot of railway personnel.

Another time we were on our assisting jobs to Sheffield, and again we had a 4-4-0 Class 2 passenger engine, No. 691. This engine had a higher boiler pressure than our normal Class 2 passenger locomotives; she was pressed at 180 p.s.i. — ours were pressed at 160p.s.i. We did well to Sheffield and did not notice anything unusual. We then coupled up to an express at Sheffield — first stop Derby. No. 691 appeared to be a strong engine, and more than 'did her bit' up the bank past Millhouses and Beauchief. She waltzed through Dore Station and Bradway Tunnel, and the trainmen must have appreciated the 'lift' up the bank. Going down the other side towards Chesterfield we flew through Dronfield and Unstone, and then, just before entering the short Broomhouse Tunnel, something unusual happened — sparks filled the engine cab, and the locomotive was rocking violently. This continued for a while and the cab resembled the sight of an old scissor grinder at work. This was about the fastest section of this particular line, and we were really moving. I was about to apply the brake, although all signals were in the clear position, and then the rocking and the sparks stopped — they finished almost as quickly as they had begun. We went rushing on to Tapton Junction, and I decided to open the regulator and carry on our way. The train engine driver had the same idea, and before we knew it we had left Chesterfield and Ambergate behind. We arrived at Derby on time and, unhooking our engine, proceeded towards the turntable.

After turning the engine, we had a good look around. Examining the bogie wheels I noticed that the round-headed rivets on the outer framing were shiny. When the locomotive had rocked violently the wheels must have rubbed the tops off the rivets. A fitter was sent for from Derby shed, and we were advised to go back to our home depot with the light engine. Our old foreman was a Cockney. 'Have you been rockin' and rollin' today?' he grinned — we most certainly had. After a lot of engine testing the foreman fitter told me that the spring hangers on one side were fractionally longer than those at the other, and this had thrown the engine out of balance. I cannot recall if this had to be rectified at the workshops, or at Hasland Shed, but No. 691 did a great deal of sterling work long after that.

It was noticeable that engines would be less likely to slip on the rails after very heavy rainfalls; it seemed that the rails got a good wash and a lot of dirt and grime was removed from them. The worst conditions for rails would be in drizzle, or when it was foggy and murky. In tunnels, it was always tricky, as dirt and water would fall on to the rails from the roof top. Water would always find its way through the brickwork from the ground above. Personally, I always felt that engines liked heavy snowfalls, as their wheels seemed to adhere better to the rails. Obviously if the snow became frozen it would be a different situation.

Finally, on this subject, just a few lines about Beyer-Garratts and slipping. We often noticed that Beyer-Garratts would slip on one unit only. For instance, working a train through Dore and Totley Tunnel, we would hear the front unit slipping and the rear unit would be working soundly. Both units were synchronised and it wouldn't be long before they were again in harmony. Perhaps when the front unit slipped, it removed dirt for the rear unit.

I should like to mention that I was privileged to drive the last remaining

Beyer-Garratt from Hasland to Crewe. The foreman reminded me that we were taking part in a small piece of railway history. I believe the engine was No. 7994, and she was going to Crewe to be broken up. Running into Derby Station we stood side by side with a diesel unit and the old and the new were perfectly illustrated. Some gentlemen took photographs, but I have never seen any record of these. Derby men relieved us as I was not acquainted with the 'Wessie' line from Stenson Junction.

I have previously described how difficult it could be to couple up vacuum brake hoses on two engines, and here is an illustration on that subject, but with a difference. Firemen or shunters usually couple up engines to coaches, but firemen mostly would couple up two engines (a driver should observe that this was done correctly). One day, a Hasland driver was working a train from Chesterfield to Sheffield; he was on the leading engine and his mate coupled this up to the train engine, and on this occasion the driver did not witness the coupling up. Later, the train was going down the bank to Sheffield at great speed and the leading driver applied the brake — still the train continued at speed —he gave the brake full application and then took it off, and to his amazement the vacuum gauge finger shot straight back to the 21in. mark. He was only working the brake on the leading engine, and for one sickening moment thought that his fireman had not coupled up the vacuum pipes. Sounding the engine whistle he looked back and tried to indicate to the train engine driver to put the brake on. Fortunately the message was understood, and the train driver applied the brake and successfully controlled the two engines and coaches into Sheffield Station. Jumping off on to the platform when the train had come to a standstill, both drivers went to examine the brake pipes between the two engines to find that one of these was buckled up. The rubber was perished and needed renewing and this occurence had, in fact, blanked off one engine from the other. Unfortunately, in this instance, the leading engine was only a Class 2 passenger type. The driver had requested the train driver to work his ejector to compliment the one on the front. When the hoses had buckled up, the train engine was keeping the brakes off the wheels of the coaches, and the leading engine was only delivering power to its own brake system. This may sound complicated but, for the leading driver, must have been a startling experience. The faulty pipe would be changed either at Millhouses or Grimethorpe engine shed, which were not far away.

There was often talk about some enginemen being 'light fingered', but I never saw any evidence of this, although stories did prevail. One chap talked about 'nicking' some paint brushes, but could have been pulling my leg. He said that as their engine was slowly passing under a bridge he saw some scaffolding. Workmen were painting the girder work and, as this chap passed by, he said that he decided to pinch a couple of brushes which were laid on a plank.

Another chap said that they had been working a troop train which was full of American soldiers. This engine crew, after being relieved, were instructed to travel home in the coaches. They chatted up the 'Yanks' and remarked about their smart uniforms. Arriving back at their nearest station this fireman said that he noticed an American serviceman sleeping on top of some kit bags. This soldier had been issued with a pair of new boots, and they must have nipped him a little so he had taken them off to ease his feet. The fireman picked the nice brown boots up as they 'bailed out'. If this was true, it certainly was a mean trick. It would serve the fellow right if they were not his size.

Some enginemen were on a train consisting of box vans, and they stopped at a signal in a lonely part of the countryside. Being curious types, they decided to just have a peep inside the first van, and sliding open the door they saw something white within. Without warning this 'something' slid across a rail and fell on top of them. They were just getting over the shock when down came another, and then another. Goodness, what a situation to be in. Hastily they pushed these objects back into the van. They were meat carcasses and these silly men had opened a meat van. They just managed to wedge some carcasses back into the van and slid the door shut, but there was still one left, lying on the railway sleepers and they couldn't get it back into the van. Without more ado, they carried it on to the engine footplate and started to bisect it. Using the coal pick or anything that was available, they chopped joints of meat to suitable sizes to fit their pockets and haversacks. The signal was then lowered for them to proceed on their journey. They hastily tossed the remainder of the carcass into the engine firebox and went on their way. It is said that beef dripping soon started to pour out of the ashpan. As their engine gathered speed, the smell of roast beef from the engine chimney pervaded the countryside. I have heard about barbecues, but this was ridiculous.

Chapter Nine

OVERCOMING PROBLEMS

On a coal train from Williamthorpe Colliery to Avenue Sidings our engine was a Class 4 freight, No. 4288. After leaving Williamthorpe it was a sharp drop down the bank to Grassmoor Colliery. The usual procedure on these trips was that a driver would slowly draw his train over the brow of the bank and the guard would be putting down wagon brakes. As this train often had sixty loaded coal wagons on, he would be required to apply about twenty brakes; he would also apply the handbrake which was inside his brake van. When the driver was satisfied that he could control the train down the incline, he would sound the engine whistle, and the guard would quickly get back to his brake van. On this trip I eased away and then shut down steam. Starting to apply the brake I seemed to get little response from the engine — she kept rolling along. We were going down the incline tender first, so leaving the steam brake fully on I applied the tender handbrake and still we slowly rolled down the hill. Putting the lever in fore gear, I opened the regulator and attempted to push back at the wagons, but by now more wagons were coming over the brow. Shutting down the regulator I let the engine roll on. The whole weight of the 60 wagons then started to push us along and we were quickly picking up speed. I dare not blow the whistle because I was hoping that the guard would put more brakes on. Looking back at this experience I realise that he must have dashed back to his van whilst it was still possible to climb aboard. By now we were really moving, coal dust was blowing off the top of the laden coal wagons and No. 4288 did not seem to be holding back the weight behind us. It was a single line track, we had the key token on the footplate, and this had to be exchanged at Grassmoor signal box. I opened the engine whistle fully — it must have been heard for miles around. Passing the signal box at speed we exchanged tokens and the leather pouch crashed on to the cab side as this operation was accomplished. Our train raced on through Grassmoor Pit Yard and workmen were hastily running across the level crossing — at this stage, all we could do was hope. If the sidings at Avenue were full it would be a disaster, and one daren't think about the consequences. Luckily, the sidings staff had been pre-warned about our runaway train, no doubt by the signalman at Grassmoor, or from hearing our engine whistle. Points were set for an empty road through the sidings, and we were soon rolling through these and finished up on the goods line at the south end of Avenue Sidings signal box. We were usually relieved by another engine crew after this trip, so when these men came along I poured out my experience to them. It was decided to take the engine to the shed to be examined. My mate and I signed off duty and, after reporting faulty brakes, we went home. The next day, when turning up for the same duty, I looked at the train board in the shed and saw that we had been allocated a different engine, No. 4294, another Class 4F. When signing on, the fitter came over to me and said that he wanted a word about No. 4288 and asked if we could tell him what had happened. I told him the full story and then he started to explain something.

It appears that when he was examining the brake apparatus on No. 4288, nothing at first seemed wrong with it. His mate had put it on and off, and it worked properly, and they were becoming a little puzzled until it was noticed that at one application nothing happened — the brake failed to work. They tried further examination and when standing in the ashpit under the locomotive, tapping around with a hand hammer, parts of the brake apparatus suddenly fell all around them. The fitter explained that the brake must have seized up in one position. We had come down the bank the previous day without it working correctly. Anyway, the fault had been found and I am thankful that nobody had been hurt or any damage done.

Whilst talking about the Grassmoor line, here is another incident with a 4F — I think it was No. 4410.

We were propelling some wagons loaded with slack from Avenue Sidings to Grassmoor for the slack to be washed. It was a heavy gradient, as I have mentioned, and so it was necessary to try to get up speed to make sure that the heavy wagons were propelled over the railway crossing and up to the sidings. We had a good head of steam, were going along nicely, and were fast approaching the level crossing which passed through the pit yard. Suddenly, there was a lot of banging and clanging coming from the outside motions. The side rod had broken off and was making quite a noise as it was being lashed about. Shutting down steam, I allowed the wagons and guard's van to run on. We were about on the crossing by this time, and were lucky when the weight of the train pulled us clear of this. We soon came to a standstill as we were still on an incline and, applying the engine brake, we climbed down to examine the extent of the damage. The guard arranged for the colliery shunt engine to take the wagons off our disabled engine. We were on a single line, had the key token in our possession, and so were safely protected.

In cases of a broken side rod on an 0-6-0 type engine, the instructions were that we should remove the broken rod and then remove the rod at the opposite side of the engine. Instead of being six-wheeled coupled, the engine would then be a four-wheeled coupled one. This would also eliminate strain at one side and would be sufficient to get the engine back to the shed under its own power. This was alright in theory, but the rod had broken in the wrong place, apart from the fact that we had no proper tools to cope with a bent side rod. We sent for the fitters who came with a fresh engine for us. After stripping down all the side rods, No. 4410 was taken in for repair.

I fired on one or two of the American engines that were sent over during the war and they seemed very similar to our own, but my driver remarked that the engine brakes were not too good. The only thing I remember about them was the whistle — they sounded like those in the American movies.

During their railway career, most main line drivers and firemen would get on the footplate of many different types of engines. Often, engines would work over the Midland line from other regions, and vice versa. When sitting on our engines at passenger stations we were often asked funny questions —

here are just a few. 'How can you see where you are going with those paraffin lamps on the front of your engine?' 'How do you steer an engine?' 'What do you do when you want to go to the toilet?' and sometimes, 'Aren't railway platelayers idle — they are always leaning on their shovels whenever we pass by in coaches'. What were the poor fellows expected to do — just stand there and get knocked down?

Once when travelling with a 'Jubilee' class engine between Butterley and Buckland Hollow, we saw a cow walking up the line towards us. Our express train was travelling pretty fast, but the stupid animal seemed intent on getting killed and just kept walking on. We were shut down, as this section is on a downhill gradient, so I opened the regulator quickly and the cylinder steam release cocks, and attempted to try to frighten the animal out of our path. The trick worked and the noise of the escaping steam was just enough to make the cow run down the bank side. We stopped at Crich Junction and reported 'cattle on the line'. All the trains on the 'up' and 'down' lines were then stopped until the animal was returned to a field, and the broken fence in the field where it had escaped from would then be repaired.

Great care was exercised when working loose-coupled trains over sections of line that had subsidence. Drivers and their guards had a good understanding as to what they were going to do. For instance, approaching these dips the driver might elect to almost stop and then, picking up the train with his engine, pull the train quickly through the subsided section. Another time, he might let the train roll along and carefully pull it through. The guard would be anticipating all this, noting when to use the brake in his guard's van to assist in keeping the wagons stretched out. There have been instances of couplings breaking over these sections and trains becoming divided. It was far better to have a fitted, or passenger train as on these all the vehicles or coaches were pulled tightly together with screw-type couplings. An old ganger used to say that he knew a subsidence was about to happen long before we did; these chaps had a remarkable knowledge of the permanent way. When the Chief Inspector felt that the subsidence had finished, he would make arrangements for it to be filled up again with ballast. This was usually done at weekends when traffic was at a minimum.

A serious position drivers and firemen could find themselves in was 'sticking' in tunnels. This occasionally happened in Dore and Totley, Cowburn or Bradway tunnels in the Peak District. I mention these because they are the ones we were acquainted with. If a train had to be divided, and a few wagons taken forward, it could be very unpleasant when returning for the rear portion. These incidents occurred when sanders were not working and engines slipped to a standstill, or engines became too low in steam. Many rules had to be observed and detonators used to protect any wagons left in tunnels in this way.

This brings to mind a trip with a chap who was to be passed out as a driver, and had a Class 8 freight and a full load. We had to pass through Dore and Totley Tunnel during part of our journey so I let him take over the regulator. This is a very long tunnel and it was about 1a.m. on a Monday morning when we were scheduled to go through it. We had relieved the crew of our Class 8 freight on the main line at Hasland, and had not had the chance to examine the engine's sanding apparatus. I suggested to my mate that it would be wise to give the engine a lot of regulator and try to get a good run into Dore and

Totley Tunnel. The last train to pass through on our line would probably have been the night stopping passenger train from Sheffield. Three hours or more could have elapsed between that train and ours, and in that time a lot of dripping water, soot and grime would have fallen on to the rails from the tunnel roof and moorland above.

This particular morning was no exception, and the Class 8 freight was soon to let us know that she was on a 'skating rink'. Young Harold put the sanders on and we charged into the tunnel. There was a lot of smoke coming off the engine chimney, as it was necessary to keep up heavy firing. When we had travelled for about a quarter of a mile the slipping got worse. The sanders did not appear to be helping us, so we quickly assumed that they had become blocked up. My mate kept opening and shutting the regulator and was trying to encourage the locomotive to keep plodding on — I should have said slipping, for that is all we appeared to be doing. The poor chap's arms must have ached so I offered to take over, but he said that he would manage; he was having his problems and I was having mine. The exhaust injector kept knocking off, so I applied the live steam injector at the opposite side. Thick smoke was coming into the engine cab and we could hardly see one another. I soaked our handkerchiefs in the bucket of water and we tried to hold these over our mouths. My mate already had his hands full, opening and closing the regulator which he found difficult; I was attempting to fire the engine in short bursts to try and reduce the smoke. After what seemed an eternity, we noticed that the engine was moving along a little faster, the rush of air inside the tunnel felt fresher, and we knew then that we were on the downward section, heading towards Grindleford Station. My mate was now able to shut down the engine regulator, the engine and train were freewheeling towards the tunnel mouth, and we could see the green signal near the end of the tunnel.

Finally, reaching the station platform, we both filled our lungs with some pure Derbyshire moorland air. Dropping down to Hathersage the train was stopped at the water column, so we could fill the tender tank with water. We both looked like a pair from the Black and White Minstrels, and on looking at our watches were amazed to see that the episode referred to had taken over an hour and a half. On a normal run, trains would easily clear the tunnel in half an hour.

Still on the subject of tunnels here is another 'hair-raising' experience — 'hair-raising' being the operative words.

Our engine was a Beyer-Garratt type, and we were travelling light engine from Wellingborough to pick up wagons from the ironstone mines at Ashwell. We had passed Corby Iron Works at speed and, hurtling down into Corby Tunnel, my driver shut down steam, naturally putting the steam jet on before doing so. Then it happened — the cab was enveloped in flames and we had a terrific back draught from the firebox, the fire hole slide doors were open and I got the lot. My driver reached for the regulator and was fortunate to find it first time. As soon as the exhaust beats shot up the chimney, the flames were drawn back into the firebox. I kicked the fire hole doors shut and, quickly picking up speed on the 'down' gradient the Beyer-Garratt literally flew out of that tunnel. All signals were in the clear position so were alright in that direction. The hair on my arms was singed off, and I was minus eyebrows and eyelashes. My mate had a good laugh and said that I resembled a plucked chicken. The holes in the jet pipe ring were obviously partly blocked, the jet had coped with ordinary conditions but was not strong enough to overcome the quick rush of air as we had entered the tunnel. We reported this, and the repair to the jet would be carried out before the Beyer-Garratt was allowed to leave the shed again.

Whilst on the subject of fire, I should like to talk about fires on wagons or coaches. Sometimes when wagon axleboxes were out of grease, the axle would overheat and melt the bearings; the grease and dirt around the box would then catch fire. The wagons would set up a screeching noise, and if this didn't warn the signalmen or drivers, the flames often would. If the fire was spotted in time, a signalman would contact his signal box mate ahead and warn him to stop the oncoming train. Eventually, the train would be stopped and the defective wagon shunted off at the first available place. When we were enjoying a good trip and this occurred, it could be a bit of a nuisance. So much time was involved in stopping a long train, uncoupling the burning wagon, and then shunting it off and coupling up again. Still, better to be safe than sorry!

It was a different story with coaches, and great care had to be taken that the hot axlebox didn't quickly cause the heat to travel up to the coach structure. When a coach caught fire, if possible it would be put into a sidings to be attended to or left to burn out. If it had really caught fire on the main line, the driver, fireman and guard would attempt to upcouple it from the rear section of the train, draw forward a safe distance, unhook again, and take the front section forward a further safe distance. The coach would then be isolated, and steps would have to be taken so that it did not interfere with passing trains on the facing lines, and the fire would be put out as quickly as possible. I bet this sometimes presented problems when it happened in lonely places — just imagine — a fire engine making its way across the fields! In cases like this, water was obviously required and this again is a reminder of a 'water situation'.

On a Class 4 freight engine, on one occasion, we ran short of water in the tender tank. Our gauge was showing a thousand gallons but unfortunately this was defective and was not showing a correct level. The worst had happened, and instead of throwing out the fire, we decided to try to get to the nearest water column, which was a long way off. Requesting the signalman to get us a good run, we set off light engine towards this water supply, the water in our boiler proving to be sufficient for us to get there. On arrival at the water column, we thankfully tanked up. My mate tried his injector and, opening the intermediate water supply valve, was amazed to see that no water came out of the overflow pipe; the injector at the driver's side was the same. We seemed to be back to square one — now we had water but could not get it from the tank to the boiler. Fortunately, we were near a shunt yard and able to obtain a brake stick. This had a round handle which, luckily, just fitted into the injector overflow pipes. We knocked the stick into this pipe with our coal pick and opened both the steam valve and water valve on the tender. Steam flew to the injector and, because of our brake stick blockage, went straight to the tank valve. Apparently, when all the water had been taken out of the tank, slush and dirt had blocked the tank sieve. The steam that we had diverted to it cleared this obstruction. There was much spluttering at the overflow and, knocking out the brake stick, we were relieved to see water running freely again. This operation was repeated at the other side and we safely went back to our train, and the tank and sieves were duly reported to be in need of cleaning.

Chapter Ten

FOG, SIGNALS AND PIGEONS

Drivers should have a sound knowledge of all routes and signals, and it was an advantage to have landmarks such as tunnels, bridges, houses, factories, cuttings etc. This was a blessing in disguise when travelling in fog or poor visibility, and far better than 'wondering' just where you were.

I have fired for drivers on the Trent Junction to Burton line in thick fog, and they could put their head out of the cab and almost knew just where the signal would be. They knew how many bridges they had passed under on these long sections; I must confess I had not the confidence to do this, but I did know landmarks that were a great advantage to me.

A friend of mine was talking about landmarks — he enjoys his game of golf. Walking down the fairway with an inexperienced golfer as his partner, he asked him if he had noticed a landmark to indicate where his golf ball had landed. This chap replied, 'yes I have — it is near that black cow in the field'. You have guessed it — the cow had moved.

It was mentioned earlier about the necessity to make sure that tank lids, fire irons, etc. were always safely fastened on to the tender, as there have been cases of these falling off when trains have been travelling through stations. Cases have been reported of irons actually going through waiting-room windows, and a tank lid would really cause a commotion. I have personally never seen this happen but, unfortunately, have seen large lumps of coal crash on to the platforms. This could be avoided by firemen safely stacking coal when coaling up engines.

The old porter at Chesterfield used to have an interesting story on this same theme. He was asked why he never swept the dust from the station platform. 'Why bother?' he answered smartly. 'I leave that to the express trains that don't stop here'. This could be a good idea, expresses certainly did create a draught as they raced through Chesterfield Station on the main line.

There was a single line pilotman at Avenue Sidings who had to walk to work on the early shift. His home was a good distance away and on arrival at the shunters' cabin he was seen to be limping. 'Oh my poor feet do hurt', he groaned. 'No wonder', one of the lads quipped 'you've got your shoes on the wrong feet'. We all gostered, but this was the old lad's plaintiff reply. 'Well if I have, my wife must take the blame as she must have moved them — I put them in the right position when they were left under the sideboard last night. When I get home I will strangle her'.

Here is a story about old Pat, at the engine shed. As you will have guessed, this fellow was Irish. He was only 5ft. tall but, for his size, was a good worker.

He liked a little nod in the sand house, and often got quite dirty when emptying coal wagons. They didn't have 'all mod cons' at his home, and showers were unheard of; consequently, our Pat had his bath in the mess room. He would strip off, and unashamedly wash himself in the large brown earthenware type sink. Soap was scarce at that time, so he used soft soap which, as most people know, resembles vaseline. At the depot we had buckets full of this stuff and, as previously described, firemen would use it to black the boiler front and make it shine; it was heavy and for industrial use only. One of the firemen substituted Pat's soft soap for vaseline, and didn't the poor fellow cut some capers. Later we came 'clean' and admitted what we had done. A 'dirty' trick, I agree, but happily it was soon forgotten — but to hear an Irishman swear — 'oh dear!'

I have talked a great deal about assisting engines, and very often drivers needed piloting over sections of the line that they were not acquainted with. On many of these occasions I piloted drivers from Chesterfield to Chinley on the Manchester line. Signing on at about 5a.m., and after reading the notices and leaving at 5.10a.m., I would walk down the line to Chesterfield, arriving at 5.50a.m. The train was due at that time and usually arrived about 6a.m.; it was a very good timekeeper and was always pulled by a big engine. This was a chance to get acquainted with 'Jubilees', 'Black Fives', 5XPs, 'Patriots' and similar type engines. It was a Dover to Manchester car special, and the crew were London men who would lodge at Manchester and return home in the evening. The train consisted of coaches for the passengers and large box-type vans for the cars. It appears that after travelling over from the Continent, holidaymakers would have their cars loaded into the van at Dover, and then retire to the coaches. They could really retire, as sleeping coaches were among the other coaches. Many of these London drivers would allow us to keep charge of the controls until the train arrived at Manchester. This was a dead end station and, when finally arriving with the engine buffers up to the station's buffers, one of these old cockneys once used these unforgettable words, 'there, you bleeder, you can't go any farver'. He was referring to the train coming from Dover to Manchester, which is quite a long way, and then running literally into a wall. Looking back to the reference about hot boxes, this very same train arrived one Sunday morning and one of the coaches had a hot box. Fortunately this was noticed when the wheel tapper was checking around at Chesterfield. The coach was put off in the 'down' bay line, much to the annoyance of pyjama-clad passengers who had to transfer to another coach. They were annoyed, but we were pleased that this had been spotted in good time. It would only have got worse, and we passed through a lot of tunnels on that run. Had a coach caught fire in one of those, I hardly dare think of the possible consequences.

It always impressed me, when working faster trains, how signals were positioned, as there had been a lot of careful calculation done. Some sections appeared to be short and called for quick reaction from drivers, but always from a distant signal in the 'on' position to the next stopping signal there seemed sufficient stopping distance. This was often discussed in relief cabins and mess rooms, and varying experiences were related.

Drivers talked about the times when they had felt tired and had difficulty keeping their eyes open, and had, therefore, lost proper concentration. They may have passed the distant signal, for example, then doubt crept into their

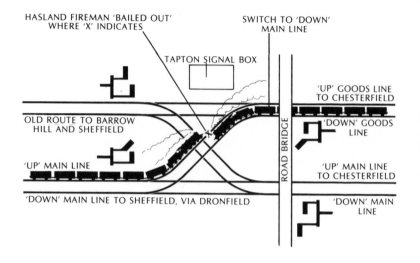

A sketch of Tapton Junction, giving an idea how the unfortunate fireman on the 'down' goods line thought that the 'up' train was going to crash into him. He was very fortunate not to have been seriously injured or killed.

minds. Was that last distant signal in the clear position and did they miss it? Sometimes they would apply the brakes, just in case, then breathe a sigh of relief when the home signal and others in advance were for 'right away'. They had, in fact, actually seen the distant signal, but doubt had got the better of them.

Guards also had similar tales to tell. They hadn't got a mate to talk to and might easily 'nod off'. They talked about suddenly waking up and looking out of the rear windows of their brake vans — then panic set in. There were no wagons in front of them — no wonder, in their half-awake state they were looking through the wrong windows (the rear ones). They were relieved, therefore, when they turned round and through the front windows could see the wagons and engine steaming away in front of them.

Here is an amazing incident that happened at Tapton Junction. A coal train was leaving the 'down' goods line signal and was switching to the down main line. At the same time, an empty wagon train was leaving the 'up' main line signal and was switching to the 'up' goods line. The fireman on the 'down' train had just been firing his engine. It was a left-hand firing type. He looked out of the cab and saw the 'up' train coming straight towards him, and without any more ado, he bailed out. This was certainly his lucky day because he landed right in front of the oncoming train and could have been killed but, instead, the 'up' train passed over him. As he lay between the rails, his faced pressed to the ground, this must have been a terrifying experience. Luck was really on his side because the day before this happened, platelayers had removed the old ballast from between the sleepers, which enabled the lad to press his body further down. A truly remarkable story, but it was related to me by the fireman concerned and he often says that he finds it embarrassing to talk about.

Firing on an engine cab at night was almost like being in a boiler house as there was not a lot to see outside. In the wintertime, with the wind blowing at the cab side, we often closed the windows and concentrated solely on the firing, being totally absorbed with steam pressure and watching the water level. It is a good job that this next experience didn't happen at night, or it might have been a very different story.

On an express train from Chesterfield to Nottingham we were stopped by signals at Danesmoor signal box. A railway inspector approached us and climbed up into the engine cab. 'There is a landslide between here and Morton', he explained. 'I have the authority to conduct you forward and show you where it starts and ends'. 'You are to exercise great care and be prepared to stop if the flagman shows you a danger signal'. We had almost reached the top of Morton Bank and could see gangs of workmen digging near to the 'down' main line. It was a most unusual sight; the whole of the bank side had slipped forward. This was grass-covered and the grass had held it all together. At the top of this bank we could see railings to the field above, and between these railings and the bank was a long cutting. It almost looked as if a giant bulldozer had scraped all the earth away. The bottom part, which the platelayers were working on, was touching the 'down' main line sleepers, and a train approaching on that line would have cut into it. The ganger in charge of this section had certainly been very alert and helped to avoid a serious accident. From the footplate of an engine it would have been very difficult to see the hazard in good time. It was almost like an optical illusion, the bank moving en masse in this way. Trains were only allowed on the 'up' line until a lot of the earth was cleared away and it was considered safe to pass on the 'down' line. In this area, it was a common sight to see the banks on fire, and being a coal producing area, there were often stratas of coal in the embankments. As with haystacks, these would sometimes burst into flames, combustion taking place. When this happened, the fire would have to be dealt with, and fire-engines often turned out to extinguish the fire hazard. Other fires, — those seen from carriage windows — unfortunately might have been caused by sparks from engine chimneys. Cornfields have literally been destroyed in this way, and hedges and trees would also suffer the same fate.

A more pleasant side to the job than witnessing things being destroyed in this way was when drivers worked trains to the brewery. After disposing of the beer wagons they were often invited for a 'quick one' by the brewer. This was good stuff and far better than the beer from the pub (perhaps there wasn't any water in it).

Incidents like these stay in one's mind for ever, and even now, after more than twenty years away from the railway company, I still have dreams about being on a footplate. Reaching for the coal pick, cracking up the coal, shovelling it into the firebox — all this comes back to me in my dreams. Sometimes I have good trips, but invariably they are bad ones. You know what dreams tend to do. The other night I dreamt about firing on a passenger engine and my mate was one of those strict-type drivers. We had bad coal on the tender and steam pressure was down. I tried everything but to no avail. Oh was I pleased and relieved when I finally woke up.

On another night, in my dreams, I was driving a train down our main road (there used to a railway crossing at the bottom for local shunt engines and the gates are still in evidence). We were racing down the road with our train and could not stop. The local shunter was just passing in front of us, the crossing gates protecting the road. I tried everything — reversing the engine — the lot. Oh was I pleased to wake up or heaven knows what would have happened.

Things around here have certainly changed over the years. The stretch of line just referred to used to serve the giant Tube Industries, the brewery, Robinson's (the quaker oat box makers), Plowright's (the steel people), the electricity works, gasworks, Co-operative, and our favourite brewery. Nearly all of these lines have gone and the old station in West Bars is no more. This served the Chesterfield to the East Coast line, and in its place is the Post Office Accountants General Department. This provided work for hundreds of people and many London people followed their jobs here when the London department in which they worked closed. They are comfortably settled now, and are taking an active part in the town's welfare.

To get a heavy train to some of these factories, we had to set back to the side of the Derbyshire Cricket Ground at the Queen's Park. When about three sets of crossing gates were opened, we would hopefully 'belt' the wagons up the sharp incline. With today's heavy traffic, that would cause a major stoppage in the town centre.

It was very interesting when working pigeon specials. These consisted of perhaps eight long coach-type vans, filled with pigeon baskets. Proper stewards were in charge, and these men would liberate the birds from their baskets, taking note of the time and the owner's particulars. This was for racing purposes; prizes were at stake and some of the birds would have to fly miles before finally reaching their 'lofts'. The stewards were obviously bird lovers and did their work meticulously, trying to ensure that pigeons did not damage their wings in an eagerness to get out of the baskets. It was amazing to see these birds reacting to their unusual surroundings. Only when the train was safely stopped in a siding would they be released. Immediately the baskets were opened the pigeons would try to fly out, like prisoners escaping from their cells. Then, in droves, they would fly high into the air and circle the whole area. They seemed to be saying, 'which way do you go?' — 'I go this' — to their feathered friends. By this time their wonderful radar systems would be operating and they would set off on their separate ways, often travelling the length of the country before reaching their destination. Just imagine, taken from their homes, transported in pigeon specials, and then able to find their way back to their own perches; no doubt, much to the delight of their proud owners. A sight that often disturbed us was to see a bird fly down and try to find the basket that he or she had been liberated from. The steward would gently 'shoo' it away, and it would get the message and try again. Perhaps those particular birds were not happy at home and were looking for fresh company. They maybe didn't intend to return home and mated in some local woodland. I suppose we all should be grateful for the war-time pigeons. Some of these were used to convey messages from the Atlantic ships, and other convoys, at the time of radio silence.

Passengers on today's trains can certainly look forward to comfort on their journeys, with restaurant cars and sleeping coaches being readily available. This is a far cry from the old non-corridor type trains. Many people will remember those primitive things. Just imagine going on a seaside excursion on one of these trains. Holiday-makers might be full of food and candy floss, but what if they were full of 'booze'. How embarrassing — no toilets available. These trains would be scheduled to stop at appropriate stations for toilet purposes, but many passengers must have suffered unpleasantness through lack of facilities that nowadays we take for granted. It was surprising that passengers often settled for second best instead of complaining. After all, they were paying for a service.

Here is a instance of 'something being done'. We were at Leicester Station, and the Controller decided to send us home as passengers as there was nothing available to work back. We settled down in the last small compartment of the London to Glasgow express. This compartment was situated to the rear of several sleeper coaches and the other passenger-carrying coaches were up front, nearer the engine. A young family arrived on the platform and the husband was seeing his wife and two little girls off on their journey. 'Ring me when you get to Glasgow', we heard the young man say to his wife. This fellow had the whole front section of the train to choose from and it was late at night and very dark. He pushed his family into our rear compartment and waved them goodbye. He would not realise it at the time, but most of the other travelling passengers were in the front section. Apart from my driver and myself there was now only this small family in the rear section. The train set off and we exchanged conversation, the children were tired and restless, but played with their dolls and tried to look out through the carriage windows into the night sky.

When the train stopped at Derby, a strange thing happened. A man was acting suspiciously on the platform — he seemed to be hiding behind one of the station support pillars, and not until the train started to move off did he attempt to get on. He was a queer character and seemed to be keeping his coat collar up to his face, and his trilby hat was pulled down over his eyes. He never spoke and the two children who had seemed to get over their early 'butterflies' suddenly went quiet. Imagine our dilemma — we were going to get off at the next station and it was likely that the woman and two girls would be left alone in an isolated coach with a very strange person. I had a wife and child at home, and would not have wanted to leave them in a similar situation.

Going to the rear brake van, I asked a guard who was also travelling home as a passenger if he could contact the train guard and get these people moved down the train. This would entail allowing them to walk through the corridors of the sleeping section. Finally, the train guard arrived and turning to the lady, remarked, 'there is plenty of room down the train madam'. 'Why, do you think that I should move?' answered the woman. 'I certainly do', replied the guard. Picking up the cases he escorted the trio down the train and I followed behind, carrying the rest of their luggage. The lady confessed that she was terrified and felt much safer when she was seated with lots of other people in an open compartment.

By this time the 'Scotsman' had arrived at Chesterfield and, alighting, I walked back down the platform towards my mate. This is the funny bit — I laughed until I ached. My mate was carrying my haversack and mashing can, and he looked very serious. 'You left me with a nice so and so, didn't you', he exclaimed. Oh dear, I thought that I was going to choke with laughing. 'I was watching him, though', continued my mate. 'Yes, and I bet he was watching you', I laughingly replied. 'You could have molested him'. Old Charlie was certainly a character to remember. With his rounded shoulders and drooping moustache he looked all the world like a Chinese mandarin.

Chapter Eleven

LOCAL DUTIES, TURNING AND ENGINEERING WORK

Two locomotives at Hasland that I will always remember were Nos. 6499 and 6500; they were Class 2 mixed traffic engines of the Ivatt Mogul type, and we used them a lot on the local passenger routes, often going 'round the houses', as we sometimes described it. Starting at Chesterfield we went 'all stations' to Sheffield, then down the old route via Eckington and Brightside to Sheffield and on to Derby again; all a bit complicated, and almost like a bus service. However, it served the local community well and was much appreciated.

Surprisingly, this little train was booked to run very quickly. For instance, the time we were allowed from Clay Cross to Ambergate was almost the same as the expresses. This was ridiculous as we had a dead start from Clay Cross Station and and a climb up to Stretton Tunnel; the expresses went flying straight through without stopping. The old drivers used to accept this challenge and, providing full steam pressure was available, would always attempt to try to keep time. They would have to thrash these little Ivatt engines and would really make the sparks fly. It is rather a coincidence, but a fellow who I later worked with lived in the South Wingfield area. He told me that as a boy he often used to watch these little engines and their four or five coaches flying down towards Crich Junction. He described 'the little wheels going round like the wind'. They most certainly did, and this was not a bad description of their action.

One such evening we were really flying down towards South Wingfield Station. We had picked up speed after leaving Stretton Tunnel, were first stop Ambergate and would not stop at Stretton Station or South Wingfield. We were on the curve before racing down to the tunnel at Crich when the little engine set up a real shudder. For a sickening moment one could almost imagine that she was running off the rails. Levelling off on the 'down' gradient the engine quietened down again. My mate was a bit of a speed merchant and looking out of his window seemed to pay little notice to the noise the engine had been making, so we pressed on to Derby and arrived on time. Whilst turning the engine on Derby's outside turntable, the driver was having a keen look around the motions. I was lighting the paraffin lamps and looking towards me, he grinned and said, 'Did you think we were off the rails, back there?'. I was a bit taken aback — why had he waited this long to pass any comment? 'She looks alright', he continued 'can't see any damage'. I often wonder if there was any damage to the permanent way in the section I have just referred to, and I will tell you why.

A train of vans was being pulled down the old route from Chesterfield. It was the Birmingham to Carlisle express freight, a very fast timed train which always had the bigger type engines, a favourite one being the 'Black Five'. It had passed through Eckington Station at great speed and at the approach to the next signal box became derailed. The engine and a few vans stopped near Killamarsh, the middle section was derailed and the guard's van and a few wagons were alright at the rear. It is a miracle that the guard was not killed. Vans were overturned all over the place and car engine parts were strewn by the railside. The cause of the derailment was that after passing through Eckington Station, a van jumped the rails, and the wheels were riding on top of the chairs and sleepers at either side of the rail until the train reached a crossover line. This lifted the van into the air. When the section was later checked it was noticed that many chairs were broken and there was a groove on one side of the sleepers where the wheel flanges had cut into them. Being a fully fitted train, where all the vans were screwed buffer to buffer with the screw coupling, the derailed van had literally been 'stretchered' along the route until it reached the crossover. It would be interesting to hear the platelayers talk about such happenings. They must have noticed some strange markings on the wooden sleepers from time to time and wondered what had caused them. Looking back to the start of the story, I wonder if the sleepers were marked in the South Wingfield area after our strange episode.

Two drivers came to Hasland from a Lancashire & Yorkshire depot. They were good pals and at first found it a quite strange when driving Midland engines. However, they soon became acquainted with them and settled down at the depot. After a period in lodgings, they managed to buy houses in Chesterfield which were side by side. It was necessary for them to do various alterations so they chipped in together and bought an outside ladder. The time came when one of these drivers decided to move to another part of the town, and decided to take the ladder with him. 'Not likely', said the other driver, 'the ladder belongs to me'. That day, a lifetime friendship was broken over a stupid ladder — which goes to prove — its a funny ship — a partnership.

One less serious incident about a driver was as follows. His coal house was empty, it was a bitterly cold evening and when he was walking home, down the lineside in the early hours, he noticed a lump of coal. Picking it up he struggled home with it and couldn't help thinking that it was unusually heavy. Depositing the lump into the empty coal house, he went inside the house, had a wash, and went to bed. He was awakened by his rather irate wife almost pulling his hair out. 'You know that lump of coal you said you had brought me?' she yelled, 'It's a lump of bloody ironstone'. Oh dear, poor old Norman.

It could be very unpleasant when working engines tender first, as coal dust would blow into the cab and one could soon get an eyeful. Efforts would be made to damp down the coal with water from the slacking pipe, but at speeds, and with the wind in the wrong direction, it was pretty uncomfortable. If at all possible, engines would be turned round on the turntable and then placed chimney first, but if turntables were not in the vicinity, and there was a triangular-shaped track in the area, the locomotive could also be turned by this method. To work trains with a Beyer-Garratt engine, tender first, was very uncomfortable. The proper description was bunker first, and the huge long rotary coal bunker would be quite an eyesore as an engine crew were trying to look at either side of it. Unfortunately, there wasn't a turntable big enough to turn a Beyer-Garratt, so for months on end they would work trains chimney first one way, and bunker first another. If they had, by chance, been stabled at Westhouses, Rowsley, or similar places, they might inadvertently be turned,

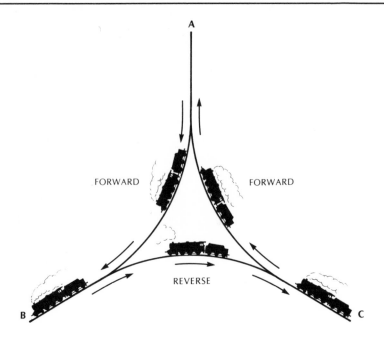

When turntables were not available and a triangle was handy, this was the simple 3-way movement to turn an engine. **A-B B-C C-A**

depending on which way they left the shed. Westhouses had a triangle, so did Barrow Hill, and Rowsley used the triangle at Ambergate Station. There were similar set ups, up and down the country, and the ones mentioned are only a small selection. To use a turn-table properly called for a lot of patience. The engine had to be balanced correctly before it would turn round. Most turntables were vacuum-operated, and this could be achieved by coupling the turntable vacuum pipe to the engine vacuum pipe. With the old fashioned push-round turntables, it was always advisable to do just that; push them around! If a driver or fireman slipped on the greasy turntable floorboards, the long pushing handles would then pass away from them. If otherwise, they might easily get injured.

At Hasland the turntable was not a big one and could just accommodate one of the long Austerity-type engines. These were the War Department equivalent of the Class 8 freight locomotives, and had the 2-8-0 wheel arrangement. They were turned out by the North British Locomotive Company and the Vulcan Foundry. About 900 were built; I think the LNER had about 200, and many went abroad. As their name suggests, they were rather austere and not as streamlined as the Class 8 freights. The old 'Austerities' were pressed at 225lb. and were very powerful. When waiting to relieve crews who were working them we could clearly hear the engines clanging as they freewheeled towards us. I well remember having one of my best trips on the Manchester line with one of these locomotives. It had snowed hard, but this did not deter her and, with the heavy load going and lighter load on the return, she never wavered.

For readers who wonder how the carriages were heated, the following information may prove useful. When coupling up to the coaches at the commencement of a journey, the coaches would usually be pre-warmed for about half an hour. Flexible steam pipes first would be attached from engine to coaches, and opening a steam plug on the footplate, a fireman could allow steam to pass from the engine, right through to the pipe at the end of the last coach. There were times when firemen have been known to shut these valves off when they have been struggling for steam. This, of course, was unfair to the passengers who would soon feel the cold. Sometimes a steam pipe might burst between coaches and the valve on the coach would be closed and then steam would only heat the forward section. Considerate guards have often moved their passengers forward in these circumstances, and this reminds me of guards in their wooden brake vans. Just imagine these fellows taking charge of a train on a cold winter's morning, when their van had probably been left standing for days before, and would be cold and possibly damp. The poor chap would have to try to make a fire in his stove; the tall cast-iron chimney sticking out of the van roof. If there was an engine nearby, he might get some fire from the fireman, otherwise he would use rag, sticks or anything else available to help him make a fire. He may even empty some paraffin on to the coal to make it catch light quicker, and this he could get from the shunter's cabin or even risk 'pinching' a drop from his brake lamps.

Leaving behind engines and personalities for a while, here is an account of something equally as interesting.

At weekends, repair work was often carried out in tunnels. These would sometimes be closed on Saturday evenings and would not reopen for traffic until Monday morning. Whenever possible, important trains would have to be diverted, and in later years diesel shunters were called to take wagons to and from the tunnels. This was an advantage to the workmen inside, as there was no smoke filling the atmosphere and making their work more unpleasant. When the wagons were in position, the diesels could be shut down and all would be quiet, except of course for the noise of the workmen.

On one of these trips we were watching the workmen, and this was the procedure. Our train had consisted of wagons with ready-mixed concrete in special containers, others with scaffolding fitted inside, and tanks with water. After taking the wagons to a prearranged position, the rest were drawn back and uncoupled at intervals. The tunnel was brilliantly lit by huge arc lamps and, on this particular evening, the men were going to repair the brickwork of the roof and also the side brickwork; they also were to repair the brickwork inside some of the ventilator shafts, and according to the depth of the tunnel, these were often deep and pretty wide. The scaffolding inside the trucks enabled workmen to stand on top of them and be able to reach the tunnel roof. Separate scaffolding was fixed inside the ventilator shafts. Men were washing the soot and grime from the brickwork with pressure hoses and removing loose mortar from the joints in the brickwork. Fresh mortar was then injected into the joints, again under pressure. It was almost like icing a cake. It might take weeks before the tunnel was completed, and if the rails had needed to be renewed, this could take months. The Chief Permanent Way Inspector would, no doubt, have a log of his repairs, and these would be done in order of importance.

Chapter Twelve

FOOLISH PRANKS, DRIVERS AND TALL STORIES

We were working a train to Cudworth and our engine was a Class 3 freight 0-6-0. We had a full load of slack and after leaving Tapton Junction saw that all signals were clear for Whittington. It was a downhill section so we let the train run freely — the engine was shut down. Passing Dunstone signal box our train picked up speed and the weight of the loaded wagons pushed us along. Approaching the starting signal at Dunstone we saw, in the distance, a young lad with his foot under one of the rails on our main line. I applied the brake but, with the 0-6-0 wheel arrangement and small engine, it was not making a lot of difference to our train speed. The young lad in front was waving his arms frantically, but it was impossible for us to stop. We sounded the engine whistle and the train rolled on. When we were a short distance away from this idiot he suddenly removed his foot from near to the rails, put his fingers to his nose, and then cheekily ran off down the embankment. At the bottom of the bank were several of his mates and they were grinning like fools. I am afraid that we could not share their joke and whilst slowly passing Whittington signal box we shouted out the the signalman what had happened. If any young readers have any similar ideas of having, what they call, 'fun', I would strongly advise them to change their minds. We are now living in the days of high speed trains and tricks like this could prove fatal. Even in the days just referred to, fast trains continually used that same stretch of line, and if those lads had persisted, they could have shortened their lives.

There is a lot of talk these days about men and women working unsociable hours. As mentioned earlier, these were part of a railwayman's life, and I suppose they still are. Unfortunately, during the time of the 48 hour week, men accepted ordinary time for their labours as being the norm; to work an eight hour shift on a Saturday was just to complete the week's work. Was there any discord then in those days? There was a fortnight's strike by footplatemen for a better rate of pay, but the staggered shifts were just taken as part of the job. It is interesting to recall one of these Saturday evenings.

In our area, we would often find ourselves on the turntable at Pond Street, in Sheffield. There used to be many old cottages in that part of the city, but these were destroyed at the same time as Sheffield (Midland) Station took a battering. After turning our engine, the fireman would rake a lot of coal forward on his tender, make sure that the fire was clean, and would generally be busy pottering about. The driver would oil the motions all around, and then perhaps the two footplatemen could sit back and relax until the time came for their departure. Sometimes they might have to wait an hour or more, and so would be sitting comfortably. The Saturday night revellers would be passing by on their way into the city centre and they could easily be heard laughing as they went on their way. There was a high wall at the dead end section of the turntable, and if a fireman was standing on the tender, he could watch the girls go by. There were more interesting things to do, however, and it wouldn't be long before the driver and fireman had company. Engines from different parts of the country would also be finding their way to Pond Street. They would be of all sorts and sizes and often from different railway companies. The North Eastern men would arrive from York, and after turning their engines would shunt into the sidings ready for the return trip. If they were long engines they would have to go up to Millhouses, as the Pond Street turntable wasn't a big one.

The scene was finally set then for something to do in unsociable hours. What better than to go to one of these 'foreign' engines and have a chat with the 'Geordies', for instance. Providing you could tell what they were talking about, things could be very interesting. In their strange North Eastern brogue they would tell us about their locomotives, and it wasn't long before *Mallard* and other famous engines were the point of discussion. I must admit that the long-distance trains they talked about sounded more glamorous than ours. We didn't have their 'Flying Scotsman', and these chaps were proud to talk about it.

Locomotives of all regions worked on, more or less, the same principle, so we knew that, had we been called on to work them, we could have coped. As mentioned earlier, we used to get relieved at York on the ironstone trains. They would be North Eastern men who relieved us, and they soon were able to sort out the controls of our Midland engines.

A section of line constantly being referred to is the Peak District line. This was far more hazardous, with its mountainous terrain. A major part of this line was underground and there were several tunnels. Here is a more comprehensive description of them.

Bradway Tunnel is at the top of the bank, between Dronfield and Dore and Totley stations, and it is over a mile long. Just on the corner of Totley is the very short Totley Tunnel, 90yds. long, and between that one and Grindleford is the very long Dore and Totley Tunnel, which is the second longest in Britain — 3 miles 950yds. in length. This took about four or five years to complete and millions of gallons of water were pumped out from the workings. There are five shafts in Dore and Totley Tunnel, and when excavation work was in progress, dirt was pulled up from these shafts. Temporary shafts were also installed at that time to help the workmen remove the rock and dirt. Water often hampered progress and caused work to be stopped for weeks. A great deal of dirt would be deposited on to the moorland, and no doubt there will still be evidence of some of this today. Further on the journey, after leaving Edale, is Cowburn Tunnel. This is over two miles long and is the ninth longest railway tunnel in Britain. When it was built, the engineers had similar problems with water, and it is said that work was again stopped because of the terrific inrush. A great deal of the water was channelled down to Chinley, and some of it was later used by locomotives; at least it served some purpose, but the workmen must have dreaded working in such damp conditions. Cowburn was reinforced with thick steel bars to help combat the weight of the mountains above. Adding together the length of all the tunnels mentioned, it shows that on a journey from Chesterfield to Chinley and return, trains would travel underground for approximately sixteen miles.

There have been many stories written about Woodhead Tunnel on the North Eastern line; this being not too far from the Midland Section. It is said that when construction work was taking place on the old tunnel, many lives were lost and the injury list was enormous, and work was stopped for a long time because of the dreaded Cholera epidemic. The old Woodhead Tunnel was finally closed and replaced by a new one alongside. We only travelled through this as passengers after being relieved at Manchester and, at the time referred to, this was an electrified section down to Sheffield (Victoria). It was noticeable that when passing through the new Woodhead Tunnel, it was lit, at intervals, by electric lights. Today that tunnel is closed and one often hears talk about the possibility of it being reopened for road traffic, but it would be very expensive to maintain and would need constant attention.

Just one last point of interest whilst on the subject of the Peak line. In the earlier years, sidings were constructed at Bamford and a small railway track was laid to carry materials up to the Ladybower Reservoir. This stretched for miles, and the village of Ashopton was submerged when water was first allowed to run into it. All the villagers had been evacuated, of course, and their homes and the church were flattened. It was on this reservoir that Guy Gibson and the famous dam-busters practised dropping their wonderful skimming bombs. Barnes Wallis was the inventor of these huge things that were able to eventually penetrate the Ruhr dam walls in the war against Germany.

One could never tell a railway story without referring to the older drivers, and there were some characters among them I can assure you. Here are a few tales about some óf them.

Old Goz used to always complain about his aches and pains, but a little more exercise might have improved his fitness. One day, whilst we were working a train with a Beyer-Garratt locomotive, he attempted to do just that. Our train was a heavy one, the fire was white-hot, and steam was at full pressure. We were going along nicely, and were easily keeping time. I was sitting comfortably and my mate got to his feet, stretched his arms, attempted to touch his toes and was doing a few exercises. I watched him with some fascination and was beginning to wonder if he had taken leave of his senses. He reached for the shovel, and opening the fire hole door threw about six shovelfuls of coal into the fire; he slumped down on to his driving seat and chirpily exclaimed, 'ah, that's better — that's tested the old muscles'. I could have fallen down laughing —tested his muscles indeed, the old Beyer-Garratt must have felt like laughing as well; she must have been insulted. Sixty six shovelfuls wouldn't have done her any harm, but six — well what can I say.

Then there was old Pam; this fellow never could stop a train in a station — we nicknamed him Pam-Pam or Pom-Pom. Racing along on the stopping passenger trains, we would be hurtling towards a small countryside station where the platform could, perhaps, only accommodate four coaches, and this usually was the length of our train. Shutting down steam, he would wait until the last minute and then fully apply the vacuum brake. All one could do then was hope — yes, hope, that the train was going to stop. If we were lucky we might have the last coach just standing in the station. My mate used to hum, 'oh, Pom-Pom have I done it again'. It was alright for him, as nearly always we had the Class 2 passenger right-handed firing type engines and I was nearest the platform, and was in the firing line from the distraught passengers and suffered.their abuse. Clambering aboard through the few remaining doors, the passengers would be bumping into other passengers who were trying to pass to the rear of the train to try to get out. If they had attempted to get out of their own carriage doors they surely would have broken their necks; after all this confusion we would blushingly set off on our journey. The guard didn't make things any better, when he gave us the length of his tongue for not stopping properly. Further down the line other passengers weren't so lucky. With a Pom-Pom here and a Pom-Pom there, we would valiantly sail right through the station. After the bewildered passengers had realised that it wasn't the express they had seen 'passing through', we would be given permission by the signalman to set back into the platform and retrieve our wide-eyed 'flock'.

On the Barnsley line, many of the local lasses got on our train to travel to a sweet factory in Sheffield. When they had to suffer similar humiliations they were far from 'sweet'. Their language — oh dear!!

Now there was old Tafty. This fellow was a toff, and he had a heart of gold. Even when he was nearing 65, and was ready to retire, he would take his turn with the shovel, and he could fire an engine. The trouble with Jack was that when he was telling the tale, he just had to illustrate it more fully, which meant that he would not appear to be looking at the signals. He might even be down on the footboards on one knee, if he was describing how to sow vegetables. I won't take it away from him, though, he knew what he was doing and had such a lot of confidence and experience. Like a lot more of his kind, he will have passed on now, but I will always remember him as a perfect gentleman.

Another old fellow called Jack was also on passenger work regularly, and to watch him work the vacuum brake on an express train was an education. He would sit in the corner, looking through the small side window of the engine cab and apply the brakes almost with sheer nonchalance. I used to attempt to 'set him up', so that he would let me do a bit of driving. On many of our trips we worked trains either way along the 'old route' between Sheffield and Chesterfield, as explained earlier. This wasn't a bad stretch of line in so far as firing duties were concerned, as it was a reasonably level sort of journey. With a Class 2 passenger 4-4-0 engine and four coaches it was a doddle.

There were a lot of intermediate stations, most with platforms to suit this sort of train, and whilst waiting for the time to depart from Sheffield (Midland) Station, I would try to ensure that there was ample water space in the boiler, and then I would start to really fill the firebox with coal. We often had the hard, good, burning type on the tender, so there was little danger of 'gobbing' the fire. Putting on the steam jet and keeping the damper closed, I would endeavour to get as much coal on to the fire as my experience would allow. Watching the station clock for the time to depart I would gradually be getting up steam in the engine boiler. There was always the risk that a locomotive inspector might come along for a ride on the footplate, and if this happened I would probably get ticked-off for my over exuberance. By the time the guard was ready to wave his green flag the Class 2 passenger engine would be just about simmering away at the safety-valves. The boiler would have reached full pressure and I had been able to keep the engine quiet by occasionally putting on the water injector to the boiler. Water would just be showing in the top of the boiler gauge glass, and the engine would be raring to go.

Old Jack would have been watching me out of the corner of his eye. He would step off his elevated driver's wooden platform, hang his coat in my corner, and put my coat in the driver's side of the cab. He would inform me that he was going to fire the engine and take a good look into the firebox. Then he would utter his, by now, famous last words; 'Just you watch me, young man; I will be burning not more than three dozen shovelfuls of coal from here to Chesterfield'. I was already enjoying the situation; Jack had taken the 'bait'. Ensuring that the brakes were off on engine and coaches and, checking all gauges, we waited for the guard's 'right away' signal. He would be having a last word with the station staff and no doubt casting an eye down the platform in case there was a late passenger. These people could often be seen scurrying over the footbridges, sometimes dragging their screaming kids behind them. They need not have worried, we rarely left any of our passengers behind on a platform.

The whistle would be blown, flag waved, and if the signal was green, off we would go. Jack would lift the damper to one nick, and this would ensure a decent airflow under the firebars. He would fully open the steam jet to clear away the black smoke which would now be coming off the chimney. He would not want to create too much smoke under the short tunnels north of Sheffield Station.

We would be stopping at Attercliffe Road Station in minutes, then passing Grimethorpe engine shed on our way down to Brightside. Outside Grimethorpe Shed we might even see a few 'namers' — *Newfoundland, Fiji, Leander* — to name just a few. After leaving Brightside it was on to the triangle at Holmes Junction, and turning right we would soon be passing Canklow engine shed. Leaving Treeton Station, Jack would examine the fire in the firebox, and by now it would be nicely burning and maximum steam would be easily maintained. My mate would look towards me and say, 'have you noticed, I haven't touched the shovel yet'. No wonder, I thought that I had put enough coal in the box at Sheffield to take the train to China.

Leaving Woodhouse Mill, Jack would throw a few shovelfuls into the firebox, and we would carry on to Killamarsh and Eckington. He would again do a bit of stoking up to Foxlow Junction. After leaving Barrow Hill Station he would remind me that he still had not used three dozen shovelfuls. Departing from Whittington it wouldn't be long before the train was arriving at Chesterfield. If the fire was still a bit heavy under the fire hole doors, Jack would rake the fire around with the rake off the tender. If not, he would put on his last few shovelfuls of coal.

Arriving in Chesterfield (Midland) Station the fire, by now, would be low, and ready for the light engine trip to Hasland for fire cleaning. Again this was only a short trip that we had worked from Sheffield, but was enough to typify what sort of chap Jack was, and how he could manage with three dozen shovelfuls.

Another driver, Edgar, came to Hasland on promotion from Keighley in Yorkshire. He was the chap referred to earlier when we emptied the coal bunker with a Beyer-Garratt. After all the steam engines were withdrawn, he taught men to drive the diesel locomotives that took their place. It was an early turn of duty, possibly about 3 or 4a.m., and whilst preparing our Class 8 freight engine, he seemed unusually quiet, but who wouldn't be at that unearthly hour in the morning. This chap was well-mannered, usually very cheerful, and fastidious in his ways. It just wasn't like him to be so quiet and introverted.

When eventually the engine was made ready to leave the engine shed, I ventured to ask him if everything was alright, or did he feel sick or something. 'No, I am not sick' he replied, 'but there is something that I have just got to tell you'. For an awful moment I thought maybe I had done something wrong, but to my amazement he started to relate a dream to me that he had just before waking up for work. It was more of a nightmare, and after waking earlier he had dropped off to sleep and the nightmare had continued. He was at work now, fully awake, but just could not seem to get it out of his mind. It had really shaken him.

In his dream it appeared that I was his fireman, we had a 5XP engine and we had been instructed to go light engine to Sheffield for a train. Just as we started to climb Dronfield Bank the locomotive, for no apparent reason, came to a standstill. We both got off the footplate to see what had happened, and suddenly the engine set off on its own. 'You catch up with it' my mate shouted, 'you're younger than me'. I took chase and had almost reached the tender handrails when I stumbled and fell on to the ballast. Picking myself up I ran into a nearby field and 'borrowed' a farmer's tractor.

By now my driver had joined me and we went straight through the hedge, up the bank and on to the railway tracks. The engine was in the distance and we set off after it. Approaching Dronfield Sidings the 5XP engine went off the track, down the embankment, and on to the main Sheffield road. We jumped off the farm tractor and ran down after the runaway engine. Just round the corner of the narrow road in Dronfield we came upon a large crater. The big engine had crashed into it and at the same time had run into some children on their way to school. Men and women were pointing their fingers at my distraught mate. 'It's your fault', they screamed at him.

Although this had only been a dream, my driver said that he was shocked and terrified. The thing that really upset him was that when he looked into his dream crater there weren't any children — just a lot of carcasses of dead pigs; it was awful.

There is a strange twist to this story, as my driver had never, at that time, been on that stretch of road, he had only ever seen it from the railway track above. Should I describe the geography of the place to him?

Well, the road was narrow at that point, it is a quaint sort of village, and the road does turn sharply and there is a school at that spot — strange, wasn't it? Perhaps my mate was thinking that he had had some sort of premonition and wondered if anything was going to happen to his family. The only carcasses that we were likely to see would be the poor unfortunate lambs on the bleak Derbyshire moorland hills. In the lambing season the snow was often still lying on the mountains, and farmers could not get to their flocks in time. To witness ewes licking around their dead lambs was a distressing sight.

Further to a mother's concern for her young one, here is something that happened in a shunt yard.

The driver and fireman were busy shunting wagons with their Class 3 freight tank engine, and a woman came up to the wall by the railside, accompanied by her daughter. The younger woman was noticeably in the family way. Apparently, this girl had been having an affair with one of the local engine shed firemen; she said his name was Brown, or could it be Smith. Anyway, you can be sure that it was fictitious because a lot of these lads were up to all sorts of tricks. The woman was anxious to find the villain who was responsible for her daughter's condition, and she was determined that he should help to pay for his responsibilities. 'Sorry missus' the shunters shouted, 'there are no Browns and Smiths around here'.

Meanwhile, the shunting engine was charging up and down the sidings, and when it was driven towards the shunter's cabin, the fireman heard all the commotion. Being a nosy sort of chap he put his head out of the engine cab to see what the shouting was all about. That was his big mistake, the two women were just turning away when the younger one spotted him. She looked up and in her excitement nearly choked, screaming hysterically, and pointing towards our 'hero' she shouted, 'Mother, that's him'. Needless to say, the lad wasn't a Smith or a Brown, but his little bit of what you fancy was going to cost him dearly.

Most firemen, like the one just referred to, took great care of their appearance; they wore blue overalls and peaked caps which were issued by the railway company, and by using pieces of wire to insert under the cap brims they could look as smart as soldiers. Some chaps would get their girlfriends to sew a badge on the front caps. They didn't look quite as smart as the American soldiers, who waltzed off with 70,000 GI brides after the war but, nevertheless, they tried. There was a safety element to the wearing of peaked caps, which an old driver pointed out. He said that enginemen should wear them at all times.

When the steam engines were moving at speed, the tender and cab would tend to sway about a lot and the fireman could easily loose his footing. After shovelling coal into the firebox he might sit down for a welcome breather and look out of the cab rails or windows. At speed, it was noticed that a man's face could bump into these things and other parts of the cab, and the peak of the cap would act as 'antenna' and help to protect the wearer's face. This sounds a logical explanation for wearing one, which reminds one of the tom-cat and its whiskers. These also act as antenna and protect the cat's face, enabling it, even in the dark, to pass along and feel the width of its body.

Further to the fact that engines swayed about a lot, between engine and tender were placed the intermediate couplings, buffers, and the necessary pipes and fitments. Over these, on the footplate, was a long two-sectioned fall plate. This protected both driver and fireman from falling between the two units. It was interesting to notice how different firemen coped with this situation. Some of them fired their locomotives 'stiff-legged', and could easily be thrown off balance. Drivers would try to encourage them to walk about when firing, and therefore keep their feet better, avoiding standing on the swaying fall plate. To give a better explanation here is an example.

Donald Carr, the England Cricket Team Chairman, used to sometimes open the batting when he played for Derbyshire. To watch him move around the crease was an education to younger cricketers. He would walk forward to the ball or comfortably step back. Other batsmen were stiff-legged, groped forward, and gave the impression that they were going to fall over.

Once, when conducting an express train from Derby to Rotherham, I watched the perfect fireman in action. Our engine was a 'Patriot' class engine, with a local name *The Derbyshire Yeomanry*, No. 45509. This young man was not a brawny six footer, but just a normal-sized person. The footplate was spotless, steam pressure was always at a maximum, and the water level in the boiler was just right. After using the exhaust injector on his side of the cab, he would walk over and occasionally use the live steam injector on the driver's side. He was ensuring that everything was working properly and, in a casual unflustered sort of way, he was in complete command of the situation, breaking up coal one minute, slacking down the dust, and then firing the engine the next. He moved about the footplate with ease, and was never in danger of losing his balance.

Many drivers were a little on the stout side, and found it a bit of a squeeze to climb up inside some of the engine motions. Engines with the Stephenson link motion inside the framing made the stouter drivers' oiling duties more difficult. They would attempt to set the big ends in a suitable position and lay across the top of the motions, but this way could get very dirty. Most of the slimmer drivers wore old macs, smocks, or overcoats for these operations, even donning rags over their heads and wearing old overalls to protect their well-laundered blue ones. This is where the 'smart' fireman could get into the drivers good books. Providing he wasn't a stout man himself, he could offer to do the oiling and ask the driver to do the fireman's preparation duties. Who knows, as a reward he might even be asked to do a bit of driving.

Driving sometimes had unexpected consequences, though! A train stopped at the water column at Rotherham (Masboro'), and the driver and fireman were relieved by other enginemen. They went forward to the relief cabin to phone for further instructions and the cabin was full of other railwaymen. Not long afterwards a guard limped into the hut with his kit slung over his shoulders. Looking round at their faces, he was heard to ask, 'who's been driving the Toton to Leeds?' 'I have', a driver replied. 'Well, take that you blithering idiot', the incensed guard fumed, and planted his fist in the driver's face. 'You nearly wrapped me round the stove pipe at Woodhouse Mill', he shouted, before stamping out of the cabin. No doubt after that incident the unfortunate driver would do his best to ensure that the guard got a more comfortable ride. Drivers and guards often signed on duty at the same depot. They were usually good pals, and this, hopefully, would be an isolated incident.

Depots were grouped together in the busy steam days, and shared the same depot number, but with a different letter. In the Hasland area these would be Toton (18A) Westhouses (18B) Hasland (18C) and Staveley, Barrow Hill (18D). Another group was Wellingborough, Leicester, Kettering, Coalville, and similarly throughout the country. In the very early days, firemen would go out 'on loan' to any of these depots, to help them get their trips in. If work was available at their own depot they would do this first, of course.

Hasland passed cleaners went to Hellifield and other depots in the north, and some even went to the nearby sheds at Westhouses or Barrow Hill. All this was good experience for the future. It wasn't always the fireman who moved on for promotion, sometimes drivers applied for shed foreman jobs, as was the case at Hasland.

Two of the foremen, Wilf and Vic, were both ex-engine drivers, and one of our guards got a position in the Control Department at Derby. One Sunday, when on conducting duties, he invited me inside. It was a most impressive set-up and was not unlike the strategic operations rooms that were used during the war. Those rooms were used to plot the course of enemy aircraft and our own. Leslie showed me how they controlled trains in the area of the Peak District and all around Derby. This caused a bit of a chuckle, because often, when we were on long hours and asked to be relieved, Control sometimes professed to know nothing about us. It would have been interesting to hear the Controllers' comments on some of the engines we used when assisting express trains. Whenever possible, the depot foremen would do their best to ensure that a big strong engine was sent on these trips, but if an express train driver asked for assistance, and he was not near to a locomotive depot, he might suffer the indignity of being towed along by a grotty old freight locomotive. On one such occasion, we had this privilege, and assisted with a Class 3 freight engine. We raced majestically past our own depot and certainly caused a few eyebrows to be raised.

There have been some 'tall' stories told about express engines travelling at great speed. Footplatemen have experienced the Class 4 freight engine wheels sliding when going fast down inclines with passenger trains. It was almost as if they were going too fast for the wheels to go round. At Hasland, the old drivers used to work an express to Manchester; this was timed very fast. One of these old codgers said that on one such trip they lost a steel tyre from one of their locomotive wheels. This was after leaving Disley Tunnel at speed. He ended his story by saying that the broken tyre was never found. Perhaps it landed in somebody's scrap yard, and the owners thought it was a case of 'pennies from heaven'. Tyres were expanded on to engine wheels at the workshops, so here was a case when a limping locomotive would need some surgery.

Another account of something unusual happening was on an express train; unusual because it was one occasion when two engines refused to start together. This was made more embarrassing because the engines were pulling the Royal Train. The Queen Mother had been visiting Wellingborough and a driver standing near to the station gave this account.

The Royal Train drew into the platform and was being pulled by two Compound type engines. The Queen Mother's coach door was stopped level with the red carpet. She had ended all the rigmarole and finished her handshaking. Waving goodbye, she graciously entered the luxurious carriage. All doors were safely closed behind her and the guard, in all his splendour, waved his green flag. Both engine drivers sounded their engine whistles and opened their regulators. Alas, neither locomotive would move — they just refused to budge. Faces started to go red and the driver on the train engine started to reverse to get the valve in the right position. 'Don't bump the coaches', shouted one fussy official. Putting the lever forward again the driver tried once more to start. Again the engine would not move, and the red faces of the officials were turning to scarlet by now, and looking at them the driver of the train engine had just about had enough. He quickly reversed, jolted the first coach very slightly, put the lever back in fore gear, and didn't he make the sparks fly. Opening his regulator and the lead driver doing the same, the two engines slipped out of the station. They were not making their expected quiet departure, but at last they were on their way.

It's doubtful if Her Majesty was even aware of all the fuss this incident had created. She, no doubt, had taken off her high-heeled shoes and was giving her tired feet a well-earned rest.

I recall another occasion with engine slipping. We were working an ironstone train to York, and approaching Pontefract the train was stopped, and the driver was instructed to move on to the loop line as a more important train was due. This he did; the loop line was on a heavy gradient, so the train had to be moved along carefully. When clear of the main line, points were put back, and the main line signal was lowered. The faster train was soon on the scene and speedily passed on its journey to York. Then the fun was to start! The signalman and guard waved their arms and the driver attempted to get the heavy train back up the incline and on to the main line. The large Class 8 freight engine had a full head of steam, and in normal circumstances was capable of pushing this very heavy load back. However, this was one day when the back sanders were not working properly. The driver opened the regulator and the engine slipped almost straight away. She continued to do this, as the sanders were not helping the wheels to grip on to the rails, and the big locomotive just continued to slip and slip. We did progress a few wagon lengths, but knew that we would have to roll back on to more level lines and try to have a run at the bank. Doing this, and liberating the pebbles from the back sanding apparatus, we tried again. With the regulator wide open and the handle pointing to the cab top, we slipped and slipped, but eventually got back on to the 'right' lines again.

At times, the driver just let the engine roar away, and there were sparks for everybody. No doubt some 'flats' were left on those loop line rails, but this wasn't the end of this 'episode'. Once back on to the main line, the driver put the brake on, dismounted and went on foot towards the signal box. Talk about sparks flying — it was words flying now, unrepeatable words. The signalman sensibly kept the windows closed and retreated to a safe corner of his signal box. This old driver threw his railway cap at the windows and his antics resembled an Indian war-dance. When he had finally blown off all that steam, he picked up his cap from the rail side, dusted it angrily across his knee, and returned to the footplate. Still fuming, he let the train slowly move away in the direction of Ferry Bridge. What could I say — nothing, except wait until the driver had cooled off and was ready to talk again.

After this slipping session, it would take my mate a while to sweeten up. It's a pity that there wasn't a sweetener available at that time.

Steam locomotive men will tell you that they enjoyed food that had been warmed on the boiler front. A tin of beans or soup was much appreciated on a cold night. It was a good idea to pierce a hole in the top of the can and so avoid the tin bursting. Placing it behind the clack box top, or some other hot part of the engine front, for perhaps an hour, would be enough time for 'dinner to be served, sir'.

Sometimes, instead of the soup tins, footplatemen would put oranges, potatoes and onions in those 'oven' positions. A hot orange was delicious when the weather was cold, and a footplateman had perhaps got a sore throat. Old Sid must surely have had a sore throat, but unfortunately, there were no oranges available on that trip.

It's a good job that the Royal Train was not the one that we had earlier shunted, as whenever this VIP train travelled up and down the country, all bridges, culverts, and stations, etc., had to be patrolled, often by policemen. We were near to Pontefract Station, remember, poor old Sid could have got himself locked up. However, policemen were not usually a feature of the lineside.

Chapter Thirteen

EPILOGUE

Looking back at 'Hobson's Choice' and the varying types of locomotives, different mates, unusual happenings, wartime and drama, I also like to think about our lovely English countryside. What a wonderful experience it was to see our green and pleasant land from the elevated position of a railway engine footplate.

Alas, there are not many steam engines left, and my favourite old Beyer-Garratts are laid to rest. Thanks to the railway preservation societies, enthusiasts can still see the fortunate engines that are being kept 'alive'.

The famous *Flying Scotsman* and a number of others are still, occasionally, allowed to venture on to the main lines. One wonders if they, too, sense the passing of time. Are they at home with the present diesel trains?

Eventually, when full electrification takes over, how will they feel? Technology being what it is they, sadly, will have 'no choice'.